D0977911

BUSINESS PLANS THAT WORK

A GUIDE FOR SMALL BUSINESS

SECOND EDITION

BUSINESS PLANS THAT WORK

A GUIDE FOR SMALL BUSINESS

ANDREW ZACHARAKIS
STEPHEN SPINELLI
JEFFRY A. TIMMONS

New York   Chicago   San Francisco   Lisbon   London   Madrid
Mexico City   Milan   New Delhi   San Juan   Seoul
Singapore   Sydney   Toronto

The *McGraw·Hill* Companies

Copyright © 2011 by Andrew Zacharakis, Stephen Spinelli, and Jeffry A. Timmons. All rights reserved. Printed in the United States of America. Except as permitted under the United States Copyright Act of 1976, no part of this publication may be reproduced or distributed in any form or by any means, or stored in a database or retrieval system, without the prior written permission of the publisher.

1 2 3 4 5 6 7 8 9 10 DOC/DOC 1 0 9 8 7 6 5 4 3 2 1

ISBN 978-0-07-174883-4 (print book)
MHID 0-07-174883-0

ISBN: 978-0-07-175257-2 (e-book)
MHID: 0-07-175257-9

Library of Congress Cataloging-in-Publication Data

Zacharakis, Andrew.
  Business plans that work : a guide for small business / by Andrew Zacharakis, Stephen Spinelli, Jeffry A. Timmons. — 2nd ed.
      p. cm.
  Rev. ed. of: Business plans that work / Jeffry A. Timmons, Stephen Spinelli, Andrew Zacharakis. c2004.
    Includes index.
    ISBN 978-0-07-174883-4 (alk. paper)
  1.   Business planning 2.   Small business. 3.   Entrepreneurship. I. Spinelli, Stephen. II. Timmons, Jeffry A. III. Timmons, Jeffry A. Business plans that work. IV. Title.

    HD30.28.T5766 2011
    658.4'012—dc22   2010047482

McGraw-Hill books are available at special quantity discounts to use as premiums and sales promotions or for use in corporate training programs. To contact a representative, please e-mail us at bulksales@mcgraw-hill.com.

This book is printed on acid-free paper.

Contents

Preface

We have worked with over a thousand students of entrepreneurship, invested in a score of companies, and created a dozen start-ups. We've worked in, consulted for, and advised businesses across several continents and innumerable industries. Our experiences have brought us a special appreciation of the value of business planning.

Some people will argue that writing a business plan is time consuming and obsolete the minute it emerges from the printer. They miss the point. The process of creating the plan is very important. The business plan isn't just a tool to raise capital; it is a process that helps entrepreneurs gain deep knowledge about their ideas. The discipline that the planning process provides helps you assess the nature of the opportunity and creates a greater ability to shape a business model to exploit it.

Will your business model change once you start the business? Probably. Going through the business planning process will result in modifications even before you launch the business. But, we guarantee that the act of business planning will save you countless hours and sums of money in false starts simply because it will help you anticipate the resources required and the pitfalls that may arise. Even though business planning can't help you anticipate every potential problem, the deep learning will more than offset the cost of writing the plan.

Book Design

This book will illustrate a proven and innovative approach to writing a business plan. Each chapter will introduce different components of the planning process. Also, each chapter will illustrate the concepts by high-lighting Lazybones, an actual company that was planned and launched and is currently operating. The key feature of this section is the comments in the margins that point out various aspects of the plan that are good and others that need work. As you progress through the book, you will become familiar not only with the process but also with the Lazybones opportunity.

A word of caution: Your business plan will vary from the Lazybones plan in many ways. While there is a consistent core to the business plan-ning process, each company has a unique story. The nature of your com-petitive advantages and the emphasis of each component of your business plan will vary from Lazybones and every other start-up.

As you begin this exciting adventure in the world of entrepreneur-ship or as you take a second look at your current business, we hope you look at this as a process, not a single event or transaction. The com-pleted business plan is only one step in the journey. There are many more steps that will have you continually shaping, adjusting, and rewriting the plan. The important message of this book is the idea that the business planning process is one of learning, growing, and becoming an expert in your industry. Going through the process helps you anticipate the future and thereby save time and money. This is a high-yield investment in your future success. Internalize this way of thinking and you will move beyond the failure rule and hit the thresholds that lead to success and value creation.

We hope you will find this book useful as you embark on your life in entrepreneurship. Good luck.

A special note

This book was originally coauthored with Jeffry Timmons. Jeff passed away a few years ago, but his influence remains powerful. He was an accomplished entrepreneur, a brilliant scholar and teacher, and a dear friend.

1 ENTREPRENEURS CREATE THE FUTURE

The weight of this crisis will not determine the destiny of this nation. The answers to our problems don't lie beyond our reach. They exist in our laboratories and universities; in our fields and our factories; in the imaginations of our entrepreneurs and the pride of the hardest-working people on Earth.

−President Barack Obama
Address to Joint Session of Congress,
Tuesday, February 24, 2009

Entrepreneurship runs deep in the American psyche. Many of today's heroes are celebrated for their entrepreneurial achievements. Sergey Brin and Larry Page, Jack Dorsey, Mark Zuckerberg, Bill Gates, Steven Jobs, Sam Walton, and Arthur Blank among others have created businesses that are household names (Google, Twitter, Facebook, Microsoft, Apple, Wal-Mart, and Home Depot). Moreover, many of today's leading companies were founded at the depths of recession, such as IBM, Microsoft, GE, FedEx, Hewlett-Packard, Revlon Cosmetics among many others. In fact, a study out of the Kauffman Foundation finds that more than half of the 2009 Fortune 500 companies and nearly half of the 2008 Inc. 500

companies were launched during a recession or a bear market.[1] In 5–10 years, we will see many new companies on the Inc. 500 and the Fortune 500 that were founded during the "Great Recession." If America has learned anything during the Great Recession of 2008–10, it is that job security is a myth. To succeed, people need to be creative in their career design, which means focusing their career on positions that intersect with market trends, taking jobs with interesting young companies, and developing skill sets that help them understand how to synthesize inputs. For those of you reading this book, the time might be now. You are not alone in your entrepreneurial dreams. Over 26 million fellow Americans are in the process of launching a business or own a new business less than four years old.[2] Ultimately, the most rewarding and satisfying careers are those that are created for oneself; create a company rather than take a job. With the current pace of innovation this probably means preparing for jobs that might not exist today. Entrepreneurs' unique experiences imbue them with an ability to combine human, physical, and financial resources to create advantage.

Babson College, along with the London Business School, spearheaded the Global Entrepreneurship Monitor (GEM) project in 1999. Today, GEM tracks the rate of entrepreneurship across 54 countries. In the GEM study, entrepreneurship is defined as any attempt to create a new business. Best estimates of the entrepreneurial activity rate for adults aged 18 to 74 in 1993 was around 4 percent. After peaking at around 16.7 percent during the Internet boom in 2000, the rate dropped to 8.7 percent in 2008, still over twice the level of activity since 1993.[3] However, not every entrepreneur succeeds in launching a business,[4] and only 40 percent of launched businesses survive longer than five years. This book is designed to help you get beyond the prelaunch stage, successfully navigate the new business stage, and ultimately grow your business into a sustainable enterprise that is both personally and financially rewarding.

---

[1] D. Stangler, *The Economic Future Just Happened*, Kansas City: Ewing Marion Kauffman Foundation, 2009.

[2] A. Ali, E. Allen, C. Brush, W. Bygrave, J. De Castro, J. Lange, H. Neck, J. Onochie, I. Phinisee, E. Rogoff, and A. Suhu, *What Entrepreneurs Are Up To: Global Entrepreneurship Monitor 2008 National Entrepreneurial Assessment for the United States of America*, Wellesley, MA: Global Entrepreneurship Research Association, 2009.

[3] For those of you interested in learning more about the GEM project and reading past reports, please see www.gemconsortium.org/default.asp.

[4] A business launch is defined as the point in time when a firm starts generating revenue.

This first chapter provides a background of the state of entrepreneurship in the United States, which firms beat the failure rule and why. The chapter continues with an overview of attributes of successful people. Next the chapter illustrates when ideas are opportunities. Our simple but robust framework for opportunity assessment is the Timmons Model.

Entrepreneurship in America

To understand what works and what doesn't work, it is useful to briefly examine entrepreneurs. We can think of entrepreneurs as falling into different categories based upon the stage of development of their business. Nascent entrepreneurs are those individuals in prelaunch mode. They have yet to pay themselves or any employees a salary. New business owners are entrepreneurs who have paid salaries and their business is less than four years old—a critical phase in entrepreneurship. Once the business has survived and reached positive cash flow, usually by the fourth year at the latest, the business is closing in on becoming a durable enterprise, and the entrepreneur's task moves toward building upon the foundation already laid.

Nascent Entrepreneurs

Nascent entrepreneurs are those individuals who report that they are taking steps[5] toward launching a business but have yet to pay themselves or anybody else within the organization a salary or wages. In 2008, 5.9 percent of the adult population (or 1 in 17 adults) were in the process of launching a business. Men are more likely to be nascent entrepreneurs then women (1.3 men for every woman) but the rate of women becoming entrepreneurs has been accelerating in the last 20 years. Entrepreneurs are all ages, but most commonly fall between 18 and 44. They tend to be college educated, but there are many who don't even finish high school. As we can see from the demographics, entrepreneurship isn't confined to highly educated men; it is an encompassing phenomenon within the United States. Granted, there are periods in life when it is more likely that a person will pursue entrepreneurship (mid-thirties), but exceptions

---

[5] Steps might include seeking funding, a location, and supplies, or writing a business plan, among other steps.

to the rule abound (Colonel Sanders was in his sixties when he launched Kentucky Fried Chicken and Mark Zuckerberg was a teenager when he launched Facebook). We often describe entrepreneurship as the art and craft of the creative, the unexpected and the exceptional. The inspiration, if you will, may strike at any time in your life as long as you are open to seeing new opportunities.

Not all nascent entrepreneurs successfully launch their businesses. Many will discover in this prelaunch stage that the business isn't viable for any number of reasons. For instance, the opportunity may not be compelling enough for you to leave an existing job. You need to be confident that the business can grow to a level where you will be able to pay yourself a salary that is comparable to what you currently make, or more. Moreover, you must recognize that it will typically take two or more years before you approach revenue figures that make such earning potential possible. There are opportunity costs to pursuing a new venture. Other flaws may become apparent in the prelaunch phase. You may learn that you lack the skills necessary to be successful, so you may postpone your dream while you seek experiences that build that skill set. Entrepreneurs often find it difficult to raise the necessary capital, and less determined individuals will abandon their plans.

Learning is a way of life for entrepreneurs. New and old businesses make mistakes and some of those mistakes may lead to failure, but successful entrepreneurs manage mistakes better. Successful entrepreneurs recognize that learning events help them reshape the opportunity so that it better meets customer needs. The business planning process can help you compress and create those learning curves and move from nascent entrepreneur to business owner. Business planning will save you considerable time and money by helping you understand and anticipate the obstacles that all entrepreneurs face when they launch a business. Articulating in your business plan the nature of your opportunity and the way you will exploit it requires you to answer many of the real-life questions you will ultimately face in practice. Indeed, your immersion in creating a great business plan will carry into your execution of that plan. You will build a textured awareness of the market and how to attack it by doing research, talking to potential customers and vendors, and generally building a network or "brain trust." In essence, writing a great plan provides the momentum for you to become a great entrepreneur, but it is *not* the business.

Even if you successfully launch your business, not all new businesses will survive. Traditionally, the failure rate for new businesses has progressed as follows: 19 percent fail within one year, 35 percent fail with two years, and 60 percent fail within five years. Although these numbers hold over time, they vary by industry and company type. We believe that you can move those percentages in your favor by gaining a deep understanding of your capabilities as a founder, what it will take for the business to succeed, and how to create ways to make this happen. Business planning is part of that process. It is a useful tool for understanding the potential, the risks, and the payoff for a particular opportunity.

Durable Organizations

Who are the survivors? What new businesses ultimately transition into the sustainable business mode? The odds for survival and a higher level of success change dramatically if the venture reaches a critical mass of at least 10 to 20 people with $2 million to $3 million in revenues and is currently pursuing opportunities with growth potential. One-year survival rates for new firms jump from approximately 78 percent for firms having up to 9 employees to approximately 95 percent for firms with between 20 and 99 employees. After four years, the survival rate jumps from approximately 35 to 40 percent for firms with fewer than 19 employees to about 55 percent for firms with 20 to 49 employees.

Growth is implicit in entrepreneurship. The entrepreneur's goal often includes expansion and the building of long-term value and durable cash flow streams. McDonald's founder Ray Kroc said, "Green and growing or ripe and rotting." However, it takes a long time for new companies to become established and grow. Historically, two of every five small firms founded survived five or more years, but few achieved growth during the first four years.[6] The study also found that survival rates more than double for firms that grow, and the earlier in the life of the business that growth occurs, the higher the chance of survival.[7] The 2009 Inc. 500 exemplifies this, with a five-year growth rate of 881 percent.[8] The lesson

---

[6] Bruce D. Phillips and Bruce A. Kirchhoff, "An Analysis of New Firm Survival and Growth," in *Frontiers in Entrepreneurship Research: 1988*, Eds. B. Kirchhoff, W. Long, W. McMullan, K. Vesper, & W. Wetzel. Wellesley, MA: Babson College. 266–67.

[7] This reaffirms the exception to the failure rule noted above and in the original edition of this book in 1977.

[8] "The 2009 Inc. 500: The Demographics," *Inc.* Magazine, www.inc.com/magazine/20090901/the-2009-inc-500-the-demographics.html.

from these studies is that entrepreneurs need to think big enough. Don't create a job, build a business.

This compelling data has led some to conclude that there is a threshold core of 10 to 15 percent of new companies that will become the winners in terms of size, job creation, profitability, innovation, and potential for harvesting (and thereby realize a capital gain). As you plan your business, think of ways to attain these threshold milestones. By understanding due diligence, intimate involvement in planning, and the intricacies of your deal, you will increase your odds of launching and sustaining a new venture.

Timeless Lessons from the Dot-Com Meltdown

Although failure rates seem to be relatively stable, there are instances where they becomes more severe. Furthermore, ignoring the fundamental lessons of entrepreneurship can lead to failure even if your venture achieves many of the threshold rules already discussed. Take the Internet boom and subsequent bust, for example. The creation rate during the late nineties was phenomenal, but by 2000, the failure rate exploded. Through the third quarter of 2002, nearly nine hundred Internet companies had shut down or declared bankruptcy.[9] Several lessons can be learned from the Internet debacle.

1. Entrepreneurship Is Hard Work and Requires Both Creativity and Rigor

During the boom heyday, entrepreneurs had visions of easy money and quick success. Television, newspapers, and magazines highlighted stories of instant billionaires. All that was necessary, it seemed, was to be young, create a concept with the term *Internet* in it, and go out and seek start-up capital. The idea didn't have to be original (how many Internet toy companies, pet supply companies, electronic gadget companies were there?), the goal was to spend as much money as possible and hope that it led to impenetrable market share. Fast growth in Internet traffic led to public offerings that created instant paper billionaires and funneled more capital for the company to spend foolishly. Venture capitalist and entrepreneurship professor Ernie Parizeau said, "When entrepreneurs become movie stars it's time to stop investing."

What we learned (or relearned) is that entrepreneurship isn't about market share; it is all about a strong business model. That means *profits*.

---

[9] Q3 Report: Shutdowns Down Sharply from 2001. www.webmergers.com.

You can't buy your customers forever, nor expect undying customer loyalty just because you gave them a good deal. You need to have a product or service that customers truly value; something that they will pay a premium for. In other words, your product and supporting service need to be some combination of better, cheaper, or faster. We should pause for a moment and explain what we mean by cheaper. Some readers might misconstrue this to mean your product should be priced lower than the competition's. While this might be a sound strategy in some cases, most new companies don't have the economies to deliver a lower-priced product effectively. Instead, "cheaper" usually means that you have a cost advantage that adds value to your customer. In the spring of 2010, Apple launched its iPad starting at $499. The iPad was cheaper than most laptops, but Apple optimized certain features and excluded others. For instance, the iPad is an all-in-one supergadget that consolidates your e-reader, gaming device, photo frame, and iPod all in one. On the other hand, it doesn't have the full functionality of a laptop. The iPad doesn't have any SD card slots or USB ports, it has limited multitasking capability, and it doesn't support Flash software. In essence, the iPad creates a new class of computing combining features from existing devices such as the smartphone and netbooks, while eliminating some features from the laptop. While the iPad may be a cheaper device, it generates more traffic to iTunes, where users download songs, apps, and e-books. Thus Apple is creating value for its users throughout the Apple ecosystem. The "better, faster, cheaper" mindset focuses an entrepreneur's attention on delivering the customer value proposition.

The business planning process is one of exploration and learning. It is a disciplined approach where you ask questions, seek answers, and plan for increasingly demanding market tests. Deep understanding and the ability to adapt will improve your chances of success. The business planning process helps you move beyond the nascent entrepreneurial stage and survive the new business ownership phase.

2. Too Much Money Is as Dangerous as Too Little Money

Failed entrepreneurs often cite a lack of capital as the primary reason for their firm's demise. The opposite was true in the Internet boom. Venture capitalists eager to invest large sums of money with the prospects of quick liquidity via initial public offerings (IPOs), poured more money into Internet companies than they could digest. At the peak in early 2000, venture capitalists were pumping $8 million to $15 million per round of investment into early-stage deals and a whopping $22 million[10] per round into later-stage deals. Expected to spend this money, many of the Internet entrepreneurs spent foolishly in vain efforts to capture market share. Boo.com spent $130 million in 7 months to launch a fashion Web site, and failed. Webvan, a grocery delivery service, blew over $800 million and then failed. The excess money insulated these companies from the market validation of their value proposition. That is, these companies used investor money, rather than profits, to sustain operations (at least in the short term). With huge war chests of cash, these companies could sell their product or provide their service at a loss, and never really understand if they could ever command a price high enough to generate a profit. Market share was all that mattered, because there was going to be some investor (usually the public market) who would pay more than the company was worth. Then, conceivably, the entrepreneur and early investors could get their money out plus huge returns. Ultimately, these companies destroyed wealth, and few entrepreneurs enjoyed the highly publicized short-term gains. Toby Lenk, founder of eToys, was worth $850 million dollars (on paper) the day after his company went public. In part, to set an example, and in part because selling a large chunk of his shares would have hurt the overall value of his company, Toby Lenk held almost all of his shares until the company went bankrupt.[11]

The key is to get enough money to get started, but not so much that your business is insulated from market tests. It is critical to learn early whether your product or service has the potential to earn profits. Your venture needs to answer several questions in the early iterations of growth. Will the customer pay enough for the product so that the firm can be profitable? Will the customer stay loyal to your company or shop for the best price? How much will it cost to capture the customer in the first place? If your entrepreneurial venture is on a tight budget, you learn the answers to these questions quickly. You then have time to adapt your business so that it does answer the questions in the affirmative. Business planning helps you define milestones that you need to achieve on your journey toward a sustainable business. Once you identify these milestones, business planning helps you assess how much capital you need to achieve them and when you should raise that capital. Devise your funding strategy around

---

[10] VentureOne.
[11] M. Sokolove, "How to Lose $850 Million—and Not Really Care," *New York Times Magazine*, June 9, 2002, 64–67.

those key milestones. For example, in developing a prototype, you may be able to use your own resources, such as your time and small infusions of your personal cash. After you have a prototype, the next milestone might be to produce and sell your product or service. This might require investment from friends and family. Tying your capital needs to milestones helps you test the concept, see if it passes, thereby ameliorating some of the risk, and then move toward the next milestone.

3. The First Mover's Advantage Is an Urban Legend

Having worked with numerous entrepreneurs and student entrepreneurs, one thing that we hear over and over is that "our company will have a first mover's advantage." Often, this is the sole critical assumption on which entrepreneurs base their competitive advantage. In truth, first mover's advantage rarely works in isolation from other competitive advantages. Numerous examples illustrate that the first to market is rarely the industry leader in the long run. A company called Audio Highway had the first MP3 player,[12] but it was supplanted by Apple's iPod. When Facebook was founded, MySpace held the preeminent position in social networking. Just four years later, in 2008, Facebook surpassed MySpace in the number of unique visitors[13] and is now the dominant social networking site. Visicalc had the first spreadsheet, but it was supplanted by Lotus 123, which was supplanted by Microsoft Excel. Being first to market doesn't mean you will own the market.

True competitive advantage can be summed up in some combination of faster, cheaper, or better. Most often, this occurs within a niche of a larger industry. Home Depot is an example. It revolutionized the hardware industry by offering a warehouse of goods. This allowed Home Depot to offer better prices because they could get volume discounts from their suppliers. This power increased as suppliers realized that they could move a lot of product though the Home Depot distribution channel. The suppliers accepted lower margins on their product. Home Depot supplemented this advantage by hiring skilled associates who could answer the do-it-yourselfer's questions. Free clinics on common projects, such as

---

[12] Audio Highway, "Audio Highway Announces the Listen Up Player," press release, September 23, 1996, www.nathanschulhof.com/ahway/news/Press/p5.html.
[13] K. Allison, "Facebook Heads MySpace in Unique Visitors," Financial Times. June 22, 2008. http://www.ft.com/cms/s/0/302914bc-40a7-11dd-bd48-0000779fd2ac. html#axzz18ffANT6T.

building a deck or installing a ceiling fan, supplemented this expertise. This gave Home Depot a "better" product. Finally, customers know that Home Depot will have what they need when they want it. Home Depot enabled its customers to do their projects "faster." Thus Home Depot has built a powerful competitive advantage based upon better, cheaper, and faster.

Not every entrepreneur aspires to the size and scale of Home Depot. Even smaller companies need to think about their competitive advantage. For example, if you plan on starting a restaurant, you might target higher-quality food and atmosphere as your advantage. Based upon the traffic, competition, and other factors in your geographic target, you may build a sustainable competitive advantage. The Blue Ginger in Wellesley, Massachusetts, has such an advantage. Ming Tsai, the nationally known chef, is the restaurant's founder. Sure, the food is excellent, but Ming Tsai has a reputation that is strengthened by his TV show and by constant exposure in local and national media. People want to be part of the Ming Tsai experience.[14] While you may not become as nationally renowned as Ming Tsai, there are things you can do to create a brand within your town or city. Try to get yourself on local TV, create a blog talking about food, start a Facebook fan page for your restaurant, and use Twitter.

The goal of this book is to improve your odds through deep learning. The first place to begin is to understand your personal goals.

Understanding Yourself

The first step in the entrepreneurial process is to understand your goals and aspirations. Ask yourself the following questions:

1. What are my career goals?
2. How does an entrepreneurial endeavor help me achieve these goals?
3. What skills do I need to develop in order to be successful?

Entrepreneurship isn't about making money (although that often comes); it is about achieving self-actualization. Entrepreneurs view their ventures as their "babies." The analogy is strong and powerful. Entrepreneurs nurture their business in the early years, helping it grow and mature,

---

[14] For more on Ming, see www.ming.com.

often with the goal that the business will outlive them. In a sense, creating a business is a form of immortality. Many of the largest businesses in the country are privately held family businesses that pass from generation to generation. Marriott Hotels, Molson Beer, Mars (the chocolate manufacturer of such brands as M&Ms and Snickers), Tyson Foods, and L.L.Bean are just a sampling of family-owned firms that survive their founder. So what does it take to be successful?

The first step is to assess what you want to achieve in the long run. We all have to work to support ourselves and our families. Entrepreneurship can be an attractive alternative to the traditional job. But just as you set goals in a traditional job (annual performance reviews), you should set goals for an entrepreneurial career. The goals should be both personal and professional, and you need to understand the tradeoffs between the two. For example, many people claim that they are pursuing entrepreneurship to be their own boss. Entrepreneurs are far from independent and have to serve many masters and constituencies, including partners, investors, customers, suppliers, creditors, employees, families, and those involved in social and community obligations. Entrepreneurs, however, can make free choices of whether, when, and what they care to respond to. Moreover, it is extremely difficult, and rare, to build a business beyond $1 million to $2 million in sales single-handedly. Thus the tradeoff is that, to be successful, you have to recognize who the important stakeholders are, but you do have final say.

Other people pursue entrepreneurship to set their own hours. The underlying implication is that you can work fewer than the standard 40 hours a week that you might have in a corporate job. The reality is that to start a successful, growing venture (one that has the potential to be a sustainable ongoing concern), you will likely exceed 40 hours a week every week. The typical mantra of entrepreneurs is that they get to "work any eighty hours a week that they want." So understand the tradeoffs going into an entrepreneurial career, because if you are surprised by the level of commitment required, you'll more than likely fail.

Surprisingly, the primary motive that drives most people to entrepreneurship isn't the opportunity to become incredibly wealthy. Entrepreneurs seeking high-potential ventures are more driven by building enterprises and realizing long-term capital gains than by instant gratification through high salaries and perks. A sense of personal achievement and accomplishment, feeling in control of their own destiny, and realizing their vision and dreams are also powerful motivators. Money is viewed as a tool and a way of keeping score.

If the aforementioned motivators ring true for you, then entrepreneurship may be the way to achieve your goals. It may be hard to envision how an entrepreneurial endeavor helps you achieve your goals unless you have been involved in previous start-ups. Business planning can help you visualize how entrepreneurship may help you achieve your goals. Business planning is nothing more than sophisticated scenario analysis to identify an opportunity, the customer, and how to reach the customer. Furthermore, you will also identify what is possible. If you succeed in implementing your vision, business planning helps you imagine the future. You will get a sense of how the business might grow. Specifically, your financial pro forma statements will suggest the upside potential of a successful venture.[15]

Finally, business planning will help you identify the skills that are necessary to successfully implement the business. You will likely not possess all those skills yourself. As stated earlier, most successful ventures are launched by teams, meaning that others fill the gaps where you are lacking. However, you need enough skills to be credible as a lead entrepreneur. You need to have something special, whether it is technical wizardry or business acumen, which can draw others to join you in your quest. One of the first market tests that all entrepreneurs confront is whether they can attract other core team members to join them. Again, the business plan will help you define what attributes those core team members should possess.

As we have worked with entrepreneurs over the years, we have noticed an internal drive that successful entrepreneurs possess. In fact, it seems that people who are successful in any context possess certain attributes. One of the authors has identified five key attributes, called Zach's Star of Success, that he shares with all his students and the entrepreneurs he works with.

Zach's Star of Success

Zach's Star of Success captures many of the attributes that we believe lead to entrepreneurial success (Fig. 1.0). Whether one is pursuing an entre-

---

[15]We will cover financial projections in great detail later in the book. It is important to note that projections are best guesses and become less accurate the farther out one goes, but they can give a sense of what is possible if you successfully identify an opportunity and execute on it.

Figure 1.0 *Zach's Star*

Copyright Andrew Zacharakis

preneurial career or a more traditional Fortune 500 career, or indeed any profession, we believe that the five points of success define the key attributes that people need to develop or possess in order to succeed. The star progresses clockwise, starting with "knowledge."

Knowledge

To be successful, people need knowledge. As the late Herbert Simon, Nobel Prize winner from Carnegie Mellon University noted, it takes 10 years and 50,000 chunks of knowledge to become expert in an area.[16] Experts, according to Simon, recognize patterns that can be transformed from one situation to another. Their unique ability to combine these patterns in creative ways gives them an advantage in whichever domain they participate. For example, the expert chess player identifies patterns based upon the current board setup and knows what moves to make next. Likewise, expert entrepreneurs see patterns in the environment and identify combinations that allow them to enter and successfully compete within a marketplace.

---

[16]H. A. Simon, "What We Know about the Creative Process," in *Frontiers in Creative and Innovative Management*, ed. R. Kuhn, Cambridge, MA: Ballinger Publishing, 1985, 3–20.

It is not surprising then, to see that many entrepreneurs launch businesses in domains where they have experience. For example, entrepreneur Sean Hackney spent several years as the marketing director of Red Bull North America, Inc., before founding his own energy drink company, Roaring Lion.[17] What happens if you don't have directly relevant experience? What if you are young, or are changing industries? In such cases, it is critical to build a team to complement the entrepreneur's skill set.

Network

A powerful way to gain that knowledge is through networking. The broader one's network, the more knowledge one can tap. This may take the form of adding people to your team, or building what is called a virtual team. If we think of the entrepreneurial process, many start-ups require external financing. Often that money comes from family, friends, and angels. These investors can add to your knowledge base, especially if you have strategically chosen an angel who has operating experience in your marketplace. Other members of your virtual team might include your accountant, lawyer, suppliers, and even customers. All of them add to your knowledge and can help in other ways as well. For instance, your investors may provide leads to customers, or your accountant and lawyer may provide leads to other investors.

The key to success is a larger network. The more people you know, the greater the odds that you can tap into the right knowledge source. To that end, entrepreneurs should have a goal of meeting five or more new people a week. Furthermore, you need to maintain contact with your network on both a personal and a professional basis. People within your network are much more apt to respond quickly when you contact them. On a professional basis, it is important for entrepreneurs to send a periodic newsletter detailing the state of their progress to all current and potential stakeholders. This keeps you and your efforts fresh in the minds of your network, and often it will spur members to act on your behalf. They might connect you with an investor or customer without you directly soliciting their help. So as you start this business planning process,

---

[17] M. Hendricks, "Do You Really Need a Business Plan?" *Entrepreneur Magazine*, December 2008, 93–95.

talk to as many people as you can, and keep them informed of your progress.

Energy

Building knowledge and networking take energy. As Dennis Kimbro, best-selling author of *Think and Grow Rich: A Black Choice*, shared with faculty and students when he visited Babson College, "Successful people make the 40-hour work week look like child's play." He later added, "If your work is your play and your play is your work, you will never work a day in your life." Launching a business takes a tremendous amount of energy. The typical entrepreneur can expect to work on average 60 hours a week or more. In reality, most entrepreneurs find that they never leave the job. Even when they are in bed or on vacation, entrepreneurs are thinking about the business. The business planning process also takes energy. A good plan takes 200 hours to complete, and that is just the first working draft. This energy is somewhat self-sustaining, assuming that you also have the final two points on the star, commitment and passion.

Commitment

To sustain energy, one needs commitment because everyone will face difficult times. Launching a business is an emotional roller coaster. The highs are higher and the lows are lower, and they come at breakneck speeds. If you are not committed to your opportunity, to your vision, it is all too easy to quit when the first low hits. You have to believe in yourself, you have to believe in your vision. Without that definite sense of purpose, you will abandon the venture when things look tough, and things will look tough at several points on the journey. Thus you also need the final point to help sustain you.

Passion

The last and most important point of the star is passion. Returning to the self-actualization theme, you need to know what drives you. What are your professional and personal passions? As Dennis Kimbro says, "If nobody paid you, what would you do for free?" If you are pursuing entrepreneurship only to make money, you will lack the commitment and energy to be truly successful. So before starting the business planning process, dig deep and find what motivates you, what fulfills you. In other words, define your passion and make sure that your proposed business incorporates that passion. The points on the star represent a way of life for the successful entrepreneur. We urge you to consider and incorporate those points into your life.

The Nature of Opportunity

Once you understand your career and entrepreneurial goals, as well as your passion, it is often easy to generate a list of several business ideas. However, not every idea is a viable opportunity; in fact, most are not. By opportunity, we mean a business that can generate profits and provide attractive returns to the entrepreneurial team and investors. Many failures can be attributed to great enthusiasm for ideas that don't have opportunity potential. Therefore, it is imperative to assess the potential characteristics of the opportunity before launching into the business plan or starting the business. The simplest, most robust means of understanding your opportunity is the Timmons Model.[18]

Timmons Model Basics

Success in creating a new venture is driven by a few central themes that dominate this highly dynamic entrepreneurial process.

- It is *opportunity* driven.
- It is driven by a *lead entrepreneur* and an *entrepreneurial team*.
- It is *resource parsimonious* and *creative*.
- It depends on the *fit* and *balance* among these.
- It is *integrated* and *holistic*.
- It is *sustainable*.

These are the controllable components of the entrepreneurial process that can be assessed, influenced, and altered. Founders and investors focus on these forces during their careful due diligence process to analyze

---

[18]For a fuller discussion, please refer to J. Timmons and S. Spinelli, *New Venture Creation*, 8th ed., Boston: Irwin McGraw-Hill, 2009.

the risks and determine what changes can be made to improve a venture's chances of success, its capital requirements, the pace of growth, and other start-up strategies.

Change the Odds: Fix It, Shape It, Mold It, Make It

The process starts with opportunity, not money, strategy, networks, team, or the business plan. Most genuine opportunities are much bigger than either the talent or the capacity of the team or the initial resources available to the team. The role of the lead entrepreneur and the team is to juggle all of these key elements in a changing environment. Think of a juggler bouncing up and down on a trampoline that is moving on a conveyor belt at unpredictable speeds and directions, while trying to keep all three balls in the air. That is the dynamic nature of an early-stage start-up. The business plan provides the language and code for communicating the quality of the three driving forces, of the Timmons Model, and of their fit and balance.

The driving forces underlying successful new venture creation are illustrated in Figure 1.1.

Figure 1.1 shows the desired balance. The shape, size, and depth of the opportunity establish the required shape, size, and depth of both the resources and the team. We have found that many people are a bit

Figure 1.1 *The Timmons Model*
The Classically Balanced Venture

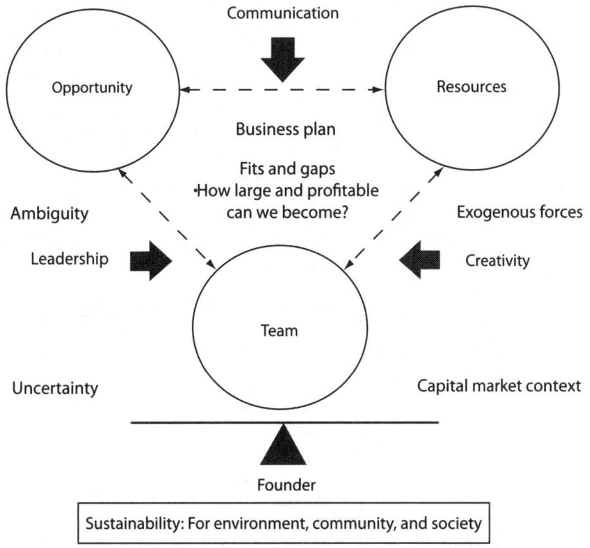

uncomfortable viewing the opportunity and resources somewhat precariously balanced by the team. It is especially disconcerting to some because we show the three key elements of the entrepreneurial process as circles, and thus the balance appears tenuous. These reactions are justified, accurate, and realistic. The entrepreneurial process is dynamic. Those who recognize the risks better manage the process and garner more return.

The lead entrepreneur's job is simple enough. He or she must carry the deal by *taking charge of the success equation*. In this dynamic context, ambiguity and risk are actually your friends. Central to the homework, creative problem solving and strategizing, and due diligence that lie ahead is analyzing just what are the fits and gaps that exist in the venture. What is wrong with this opportunity? What is missing? What good news and favorable events can happen, as well as the adverse? What has to happen to make it attractive and a fit for you? What market, technology, competitive, management, and financial risks can be reduced or eliminated? What can be changed to make this happen? Who can change it? What are the least resources necessary to grow the business the farthest? Is this the right team? By implication, if one can determine these answers and make the necessary changes by figuring out how to fill the gaps and improve the fit and attract key players who can add such value, then the odds for success rise significantly. Typically the Timmons Model starts by looking more like Figure 1.2.

Figure 1.2 *Timmons Model of Lazybones*

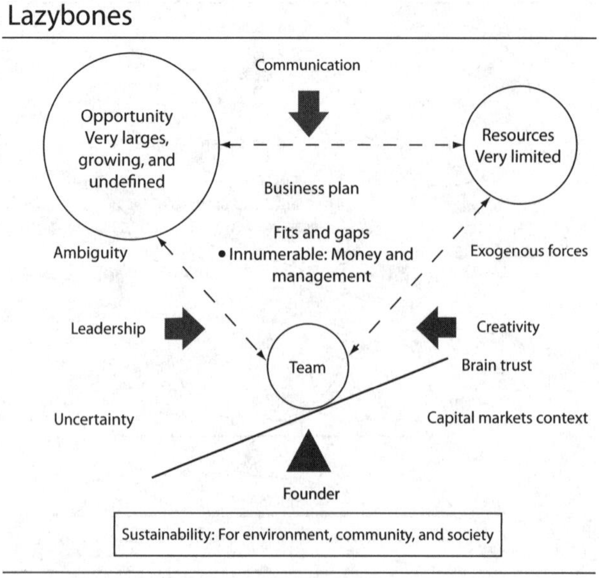

Figure 1.3 *The Opportunity*

The Entrepreneurial Process Is Opportunity Driven

Market demand is a key ingredient to measuring an opportunity:
- Customer payback less than one year?
- Do market share and growth potential equal 20 percent annual growth and is it durable?[19]
- Is the customer reachable?

Market structure and size:
- Emerging and/or fragmented?
- $50 million or more, with a $1 billion potential?
- Proprietary barriers to entry?

Margin analysis helps differentiate an opportunity from an idea:
- Low cost provider (40 percent gross margin)?
- Low capital requirement versus the competition?
- Break even in one to two years?

In essence, the entrepreneur's role is to manage and redefine the risk-reward equation.

The Opportunity

At the heart of the process is the opportunity. Successful entrepreneurs and investors know that a good idea is not necessarily a good opportunity. In fact, for every 100 ideas presented to investors in the form of a business plan or proposal of some kind, usually only 1 or sometimes 2 or 3 ever get funded. Over 80 percent of those rejections occur in the first few minutes; another 10 to 15 percent are rejected after investors have read the business plan carefully. Less than 10 percent attract enough interest to merit thorough due diligence and investigation over several weeks, and even months. These are very slim odds. Would-be entrepreneurs chasing ideas that are going nowhere have wasted countless hours and days. An important skill, therefore, as an entrepreneur or an investor, is to be able to quickly evaluate whether serious potential exists, and to decide how much time and effort to invest.

Figure 1.3 summarizes the most important characteristics of good opportunities. Underlying market demand drives the value creation potential because of the value-added properties of the product or service; the

---

[19]"Durability of an opportunity" is a widely misunderstood concept. In entrepreneurship, durability is when the investor gets her money back plus a market or better return on investment.

market's size and 20-plus percent growth potential, the economics of the business, particularly robust margins (40 percent or more); and free cash flow characteristics.

In short, the greater the growth, size, durability, and robustness of the gross and net margins and free cash flow, the greater the opportunity. The more *imperfect* the market, the greater the opportunity. The greater the rate of change, the discontinuities, and chaos, the greater is the opportunity. The greater the inconsistencies in existing service and quality, in lead times and lag times, and the greater the vacuums and gaps in information and knowledge, the greater is the opportunity.

Resources: Creative and Parsimonious

One of the most common misconceptions among untried entrepreneurs is that you must first have all the resources in place, especially the money, to succeed with a venture. Thinking money first is a big mistake. Money follows high-potential opportunities conceived of and led by a strong management team. Investors have bemoaned for years that there is too much money chasing too few deals. In other words, there is a shortage of quality entrepreneurs and opportunities, not money. Successful entrepreneurs devise ingeniously creative and stingy strategies to marshal and gain control of resources (Fig. 1.4). Surprising as it may sound, investors and successful entrepreneurs often say one of the worst things that can happen to an entrepreneur is to have *too much money too early*.

Bootstrapping is a way of life in entrepreneurial companies and can create a significant competitive advantage. Doing more with less is a powerful competitive weapon. Successful entrepreneurs try to minimize and control resources, not necessarily own them. Whether it is assets for the

Figure 1.4 *Understand and Marshal Resources, Don't Be Driven by Them*

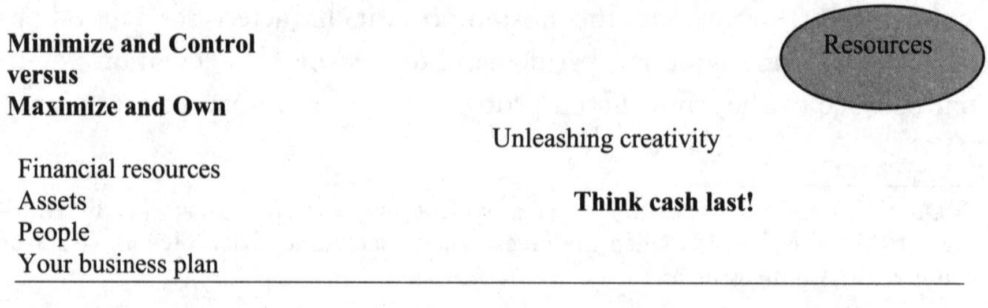

**Minimize and Control
versus
Maximize and Own**

Financial resources
Assets
People
Your business plan

Resources

Unleashing creativity

Think cash last!

business, key people, the business plan, or start-up and growth capital they *think cash last.* Such strategies have a wondrous effect on the company in two ways: a discipline of leanness permeates the firm, and everyone knows that every dollar counts; and the principle Conserve Your Equity (CYE) becomes a way of maximizing shareholder value.

The Entrepreneurial Team

There is little dispute today that the entrepreneurial team is a key ingredient in the higher potential venture. According to entrepreneur Guy Kawasaki, "the most important characteristic . . . [of an] entrepreneurial team . . . [is] being infected with a love for what the team is doing. It's not work experience or educational background. I would pick an Apple II repair department engineer over a Ph.D. from MIT if he 'gets it,' loves it, and wants to change the world with it."[20] Venture capitalist John Doerr reaffirms father of American venture capital General George Doriot's dictum: "I prefer a Grade A entrepreneur and team with a Grade B idea, over a Grade B team with a Grade A idea." Doerr stated, "In the world today, there's plenty of technology, plenty of entrepreneurs, plenty of money, plenty of venture capital. What's in short supply is great teams. Your biggest challenge will be building a great team."[21] Famous investor Arthur Rock articulated the importance of the team over two decades ago. He put it this way: "If you can find good people, they can always change the product. Nearly every mistake I've made has been I picked the wrong people, not the wrong idea."[22] Finally, as we saw earlier, the ventures with more than 20 employees and $2 million to $3 million in sales were much more likely to survive and prosper. In the vast majority of cases, it is very difficult to grow beyond this without a team of two or more key contributors.

Figure 1.5 depicts the important aspects of the team. Make no mistake about it, these teams invariably are formed and led by a very capable entrepreneurial leader whose track record exhibits both accomplishments and several qualities that the team must possess. A pacesetter and culture-creator, the lead entrepreneur is central to the team as both a player and a coach. The ability and skill in attracting other key management members and then building the team is one of the most valued capabilities investors

---

[20]Guy Kawasaki Blog, January 4, 2006, blog.guykawasaki.com/2006/01/the_art_of_intr.html#axzz0l9v7iSJ2.
[21]*Fast Company,* February–March 1997, 84.
[22]Arthur Rock, "Strategy vs. Tactics from a Venture Capitalist," *Harvard Business Review,* November–December 1987, 63–67.

Figure 1.5   *An Entrepreneurial Team Is the Key Ingredient for Success*

An entrepreneurial leader
- Learns and teaches faster and better
- Deals with adversity and is resilient
- Exhibits integrity, dependability, and honesty
- Builds entrepreneurial culture and organization
- Possesses the qualities identified in Zach's Star of Success

Quality of team
- Relevant experience and track record
- Motivation to excel
- Commitment, determination, and persistence
- Tolerance of risk, ambiguity, and uncertainty
- Creativity
- Team locus of control
- Adaptability
- Opportunity obsession
- Leadership
- Communication

look for. The founder who becomes the leader does so by building heroes in the team. A leader adapts a philosophy that rewards success and supports honest failure, shares the wealth with those who help create it, and sets high standards for both performance and conduct.

Importance of Fit and Balance

Rounding out the model of the three driving forces is the concept of fit and balance between and among these forces. Note that the team is positioned at the bottom of the triangle in the Timmons Model (see Fig. 1.1). Imagine the founder, entrepreneurial leader of the venture, standing on a large ball, grasping the triangle over her head. The challenge is to balance the balls above her head, without toppling off. This imagery is helpful in appreciating the constant balancing act since leader, team, and resources rarely match. When envisioning a company's future using this imagery, the entrepreneur can ask herself, what pitfalls will I encounter to get to the next boundary of success? Will my current team be large enough, or will we be over our heads if the company grows 30 percent over the next two years? Are my resources sufficient (or too abundant)? Vivid examples of the failure to maintain a balance are everywhere, such as when large companies throw too many resources at a weak, poorly defined opportunity.

Business planning helps you tie together the three spheres of the Timmons Model. The planning process helps you shape the opportunity and understand its full potential. Then the lead entrepreneur has a sense of what other team members are needed to fill out the venture's skill set and also the resources that will be needed to fully execute the opportunity. Examine your idea. Does it have the makings of a strong opportunity?

Scale of the Opportunity

Opportunities come in different shapes and sizes. Some opportunities are massive and may lead to entrepreneurial companies that change an industry, if not the world. For instance, through years of study, we have found that the largest opportunities occur in emerging or fragmented industries. Technology, such as the Internet, telecom, biotechnology, Web 2.0, and so forth, often creates new emerging industries. Within these spaces, demand exceeds supply, and multiple new entrants are racing to develop the dominant platform or structure. For example, the early days of the desktop computer saw hundreds of companies competing with their product offerings. The DOS-based PCs became the dominant platform, with Apple's operating system a distant second. All other PC platforms disappeared as well as the companies that promoted them. We have seen similar races in the Internet, telecom, and other technology arenas. These races are often about market share (and, it is hoped, foreseeable profit). Emerging industries often have attractive gross profit margins, allowing the companies to grow and adapt their business models (even though operating margins can be low or negative in early years). As the dominant platforms develop, the industry transforms to a mature state, and the gross margins decrease. Competition becomes more intense, and it is more difficult for new ventures to enter successfully. Therefore, some of the best opportunities for new ventures are in emerging industries.

Fragmented industries also provide strong opportunities. A fragmented industry is characterized by many small mom-and-pop competitors, each with a narrow geographic focus. Consider Home Depot. Before their entrance into hardware, many small, local hardware stores could be found. In one of the author's hometowns just outside of Boston, there were three hardware stores for a town with 12,000 residents. Today, only one remains, and it has affiliated with Ace Hardware. These large box stores, such as Home Depot, Wal-Mart, and Staples, have revolutionized retail by rolling up industries. Moving large volumes of product allows these entrepreneurial ventures to earn large profits even if their gross margins are less than might be experienced in emerging industries.

The size and magnitude of these opportunities draw in professional equity investors such as venture capitalists. An entrepreneur ends up with a lower percentage of the equity, but if all goes well, a much higher return. That being said, you may decide that a high-potential venture isn't for you. Your passion may reside in an opportunity that doesn't have the large upside discussed earlier. You may not have the skills to manage such an undertaking. You may be like the vast majority of America's entrepreneurs who are pursuing what is called a "lifestyle" opportunity.

The difference between lifestyle and high-potential ventures is a function of growth potential. Examples of lifestyle firms would include single-establishment restaurants, dry cleaners, or self-consultant businesses. Although lifestyle firms may not make you a billionaire, many can help you become a millionaire. In fact, owning a small business such as dry cleaning has generated more millionaires than high-flying Internet start-ups. Furthermore, many lifestyle entrepreneurs transition their firms into foundation firms. An example of this might be expanding beyond a single restaurant to five or more restaurants. The size of the opportunity has become larger as well as increasing potential returns. Whatever size of opportunity you wish to pursue is a function of your vision and career objectives, but if you are interested in a larger opportunity, keep that in mind from the outset.

Chapter 1 has provided background on entrepreneurship. You are about to embark on a journey that will have you joining the entrepreneurial revolution that is sweeping the country. As you begin the business planning process, keep in mind your goals, and work to identify opportunities. The subsequent chapters will go into preplanning and the actual construction of the business plan in great detail. As you read the chapters, we will be tracking Dan Hermann and his company, Lazybones. Put yourself in his position. Do you think he has an opportunity? Would you shape it the same way he has? Is his planning process giving him the learning he will need to be successful? Every entrepreneur will reach different conclusions, but the planning process is designed to help you pull together the information you need to make strong decisions.

2 BEFORE YOU START PLANNING, ASK THE RIGHT QUESTIONS

There are a number of activities that need work before you start planning. First, you do not want to expend lots of time on every idea that you might be considering. Your time will be best spent on the ideas that have the biggest potential and the greatest chance for success. This chapter presents you with the Quick Screen tool. This method can help you quickly evaluate several ideas and decide which one is the most attractive opportunity. Once you've identified that opportunity, the next step is to start detailing action items that you need to complete in preparation for the planning. We provide you with a business planning guide that will help you schedule the tasks at hand. The chapter concludes with an overview of the business planning process and the three different types of plans that entrepreneurs commonly use.

The Quick Screen

Time is the ultimate ally and enemy of the entrepreneur. The harsh reality is that you will not have enough time in a quarter, a year, or a decade to pursue all the ideas for businesses you and your team can think of. Perhaps the cruelest part of the paradox is that you have to find and make the time for the good ones. To complicate the paradox, we argue that *you do not have a strategy until you are saying no to lots of opportunities!* This demand is part of the punishing and rewarding Darwinian act of entrepreneurship: many will try; many will fail; some will succeed; and a few will excel. There are about 23 million firms in the United States. A vast majority are very small businesses with one to five employees.[1] In 2009 about 6.8 million new enterprises of all kinds were launched in the United States, or more than 550,000 each month.[2] Of those, only 10 to 15 percent will prove to be good opportunities that will achieve sales of $1 million or more. More thoughtful planning will mean a better chance of being in the 10 to 15 percent who not only succeed, but thrive.

Recognizing that you can't do thorough business planning for each and every idea you think has merit, it is important to quickly screen ideas to determine which ones deserve more attention. The Quick Screen is a tool that can help you weed out poor ideas quickly. Opportunities consist of "Four Anchors."

1. They create or add significant value to a customer or end-user.
2. They do so by solving a significant problem, or meeting a significant want or need, for which someone is willing to pay a premium.
3. They therefore have robust market, margin, and money-making characteristics: large enough ($50 million+), high growth (20 percent+), high margins (40 percent+), and strong and early free cash flow (recurring revenue, low assets, and working capital), high profit potential (10 to 15 percent+ after tax), and they offer attractive investor realizable returns (IRRs) (25 to 30 percent+ IRR).
4. They are a good *fit* with the founder(s) and management team at the time and in the marketplace and with the *risk-reward* balance.

If most sophisticated private equity investors and venture capitalists invest in only one to five out of every hundred ideas, then one can see how important it is to focus on a few superior ideas. The ability to quickly and efficiently reject ideas is a very important component of an entrepre-

---

[1]www.census.gov/epcd/www/smallbus.html, accessed August 23, 2010.
[2]The Kauffman Foundation, "Despite Recession, U.S. Entrepreneurial Activity Rises in 2009 to Highest Rate in 14 Years, Kauffman Study Shows," press release May 20, 2010, www.kauffman.org/newsroom/despite-recession-us-entrepreneurial-activity-rate-rises-in-2009.aspx, accessed August 23, 2010.

neurial mind-set. The Quick Screen should enable you in an hour or so to conduct a preliminary review and evaluation of an idea. Unless the idea has, or you are confident it can be molded and shaped so that it has, the Four Anchors, you will waste a lot of time on a lower-potential idea. The next section introduces you to Lazybones and then illustrates the use of the Quick Screen by analyzing the Lazybones opportunity. A blank copy of the Quick Screen for your own use is found in Appendix 1.[3]

What Is Lazybones?

Lazybones is a laundry service for college students. Dan Hermann and Reg Mathelier, the founders of Lazybones, were roommates at the University of Wisconsin at Madison. Like many young men in college, household chores, such as doing the laundry, were far down their priority list. Thus much of the time they were wearing clothes that were a bit ripe. A close friend took note and offered to do their laundry in exchange for a small fee. Dan and Reg took their friend up on the offer and soon were wearing presentable clothes. As graduation approached in May 1993, Dan and Reg needed jobs, but neither saw himself in a corporate position. They both had an urge to start their own company; they just needed an idea. The inspiration came from an unlikely place— their own personal negligence. The two friends started to realize that if they had bemoaned doing their laundry, so too would many of the thousands of undergraduate students at their alma mater, the University of Wisconsin.

With a rudimentary business plan, the two launched Lazybones. They opened up a laundry facility (store) and began to sell their laundry service. The first several years were a struggle. Dan and Reg worked around the clock, and they were constantly on the verge of going out of business. They often used credit cards to finance the business over the first few years, especially during the summer when the business basically came to a halt as students returned home. Fortunately, Dan and Reg found a complementary summer business to ease the cash flow drought. While school was out of session, Lazybones stored student possessions (such as TVs, furniture, etc.) that the students did not want to lug home and back. Three years passed before either founder took home any salary, but by

---

[3]You may also access an electronic version of the Quick Screen at http://businessplansthatwork.groupsite.com.

year five they were turning a profit. The whole process was an exercise in logistics, with a steep learning curve.

Six years into the business, Reg and Dan decided it was time to expand. After a friend conducted some market research, they identified Syracuse University as an ideal fit; the school charged a high tuition and possessed a large student base with an adequate amount of disposable income. Dan moved to Syracuse to oversee the opening. They soon received an endorsement from the school, which set up a direct pipeline to acquiring customers. Within a year and a half, the new location was breaking even. Eventually, Dan and Reg were able to get the business to the point where it required only 25 hours per week from them, respectively. At this stage, Lazybones was teetering between a lifestyle business and a growing business. With time on his hands, Dan decided he needed to figure out how to expand the company.

In September 2003, Dan started in the part-time, evening MBA program at Babson College. Through his coursework, Dan's entrepreneurial spirit was sparked again. Now living in the Boston area, Dan decided to oversee the opening of a local outlet in August 2008. This new facility would service Boston-area universities, such as Boston University and Babson College. In addition, Dan and Reg decided that it was time to take a risk and test the company's potential to grow. Through careful research, they decided to open an operation in Boulder to service the University of Colorado. With four company-owned stores, Dan started thinking about how he could grow their business further. It would require some deep thinking, and Dan embarked upon a planning process to take the business to the next level.

A Quick Screen of Lazybones

Just about a year prior to the Boston and Boulder openings, Dan met Joel Pedlikin during an MBA evening course at Babson. They developed a friendship, but it was not until they learned about franchising, through a finance course, that Joel's interest in joining the company peaked. During their entrepreneurship class in the fall of 2008 Dan and Joel solidified their goal to grow Lazybones, which was now in its 15th year of operation. With Reg's full support, Dan and Joel thoroughly explored franchising and the role it could play in growing Lazybones. The possibility of expanding the business to the point at which they could sell it intrigued them. The pair worked on a business plan during their

Exercise 1.1   *Quick Screen: Lazybones*

I. Market- and Margin-Related Issues

Criterion	Higher Potential	Lower Potential	Comments
Need/want/ problem	⟨Identified⟩	Unfocused	Lazybones has proven that college students at more expensive colleges are willing to pay for a laundry service.
Customers	Reachable and receptive	Unreachable/ loyal	Reaching the students is easier if the university endorses the concept (as is the case at Syracuse and Wisconsin) because they include advertisements in the university initiation packets sent to students before they enroll. It is more difficult if the university doesn't endorse the service.
Payback to users	⟨<One year⟩	>Three years	Immediate. Students have one less chore to worry about and Mom and Dad are happy their kids are in clean clothes.
Value added or created	⟨IRR 40% +⟩	⟨IRR<20%⟩	Depends on how likely the university is to endorse the service. If Lazybones is endorsed, it acquires new customers rapidly. This should lead to a higher IRR.
Market size	$50–$100 million	⟨<$10 million or >1 bil.⟩	Estimate that the university service market is $1 billion
Market growth rate	+20%	⟨<20%, contracting⟩	Flat. Revenues actually declined in the industry for 2009, although much of the decline is attributable to the recession. As the economy recovers, people are likely to increase their use of services.
Gross margin	⟨40%+ and durable⟩	<20% and fragile	Gross margins have proven to be robust, but the key is to get a unit up to capacity quickly.

Overall Potential:

1. Market	Higher _____ XXX avg _____ lower		Has strong promise as long as franchisees are located near the right type of universities.
2. Margins	Higher _____ XXX avg _____ lower		

(continued)

Exercise 1.1 *Quick Screen: Lazybones (continued)*

II. Competitive Advantages

	Higher Potential	Lower Potential	Comments
Fixed and variable costs	Lowest >>>>XXX>>>>Higher		Higher fixed costs to build out the laundry facilities.
Degree of control			
Prices and cost	Stronger >>XXX>>>>Weaker		Low price elasticity. Students are willing to pay a premium to have laundry done for them.
Channels of supply and distribution	Stronger >>XXX>>>>Weaker		Channels have limited power. Equipment and detergent are commodities.
Barriers to entry	Stronger >>>>>XXX>>None		Low barriers. The industry is highly fragmented. The only barrier is the cost to set up the laundry facility.
Proprietary advantage	Stronger >>>>>>>>XXX>None		Advantage is tied up in processes. Lazybones has tight control processes that insure quality and reliability. May be hard to replicate.
Lead time advantage (product, technology, people, resources, location)	Stronger >>XXX>>>>>>>None		While a competitor could set up a laundry service relatively quickly, Lazybones has years of experience in setting up efficient operations and developing relationships with universities. This would take competitors time to imitate.
Service chain Contractual advantage	Stronger >>>>>>>>XXX>Weaker		Potentially strong considering their record on getting university endorsements. Also, as they grow the chain, they may have supply advantages for equipment, detergents, etc.
Contacts and networks	Stronger >>XXX>>>>>>>Weaker		Founders have almost 20 years experience in the industry.

	Overall Potential			Comments
	Higher	avg	lower	Lazybones competes in a crowded marketplace against coin-operated outlets and other laundry services. They've found a niche (universities) and a model to capture that niche that has been proven at its company stores. With four company stores operating successfully, they now think they can create a franchise system.
1. Costs	Higher __X__	avg	_____lower	
2. Channel	Higher _____	avg __X__	lower	
3. Barriers to entry	Higher _____	avg __X__	lower	
4. Timing	Higher __X__	avg	_____lower	

III. Value Creation and Realization Issues

	Higher Potential	Lower Potential	Comments
Profit after tax	10–15% or more and durable	<5%; fragile	With strong execution and operating systems, Lazybones is consistently profitable.
Time to Break-even	<2 years	> 3 years	Quicker if Lazybones gets university endorsements.
Time to positive cash flow	<2 years	>3 years	Again, dependent on endorsement.
ROI potential	40–70% +, durable	<20%, fragile	Predict ~35% Return on equity by year five.
Value	High strategic value	Low strategic value	If Lazybones growth plan succeeds, it will be an attractive acquisition.
Capitalization requirements	Low-moderate; Fundable	very high; difficult to fund	Using franchising for growth greatly reduces the needs for outside investment.
Exit mechanism	IPO (initial public offering), acquisition	undefined; illiquid investment	The IPO market has struggled since the dot-com meltdown and has been hurt again by the 2008 recession. An acquisition is a stronger possibility, especially if they grow the number of locations, proving that the model works in multiple locations and develop a national brand.

Overall Value Creation Potential		Comments
1. Timing	Higher _____ avg __X__ lower	Professionalizing a fragmented market could create lots of value. Lazybones has a strong platform on which to pursue this avenue.
2. Profit/free cash flow	Higher __X__ avg _____ lower	
3. Exit/liquidity	Higher __X__ avg _____ lower	

IV. Overall Potential

	Go	No Go	Go, if ...	Comments
1. Margins and Markets	X			Professionalizing this market is promising.
2. Competitive Advantages	X			Refined unit operations are replicable in franchise model
3. Value creation and realization	X			Several inquiries from potential franchisees

(continued)

Exercise 1.1 *Quick Screen: Lazybones (continued)*

IV. Overall Potential

	Go	No Go	Go, if ...	Comments
4. Fit: "O" + "R" + "T"	X			Strong base in founding team
5. Risk–reward balance	X			Dan needs to take this business to the next level
6. Timing			X	Tough market, but Lazybones has professional business model that others in industry lack
7. Other compelling issues: must know or likely to fail a. How many company stores do we need to prove model before franchising? b. How do we identify the right franchisee? c. What kind of training do franchisees need? d. What universities should we target going forward?				

entrepreneurship class to investigate the feasibility of a franchising growth plan.

As we look at the Quick Screen for Lazybones, remember that this is an initial investigation as to whether the franchising idea is an opportunity to grow a large profitable business. When you complete the Quick Screen you are giving a best, first assessment of the key criteria highlighted in the Quick Screen. You should be doing Quick Screens for multiple ideas so don't spend an inordinate amount of time trying to come up with precise estimates (e.g., market size). For example, Lazybones might investigate franchising the concept (as Dan and Joel are currently thinking), raising external financing and opening more company stores (a model similar to Starbucks), adding more services in a particular unit geared toward needs of their customers, and so on. Understanding how one idea for growth compares with others will allow you to devote more time to refining the estimates and starting the business planning process. Every plan has its own flavor and objectives; however, this exercise should help to clarify your thinking during your own planning process. It should also help to establish embedded processes as you forge a company that focuses on the nature of the opportunity. To illustrate the dynamic nature of opportunities, we illustrate in ovals Dan and Joel's original assessment on certain criteria (market size and margins) and how some changes to their original vision have improved the nature of the opportunity.

All new venture ideas rest on several critical assumptions that will either make or break the business. As you view the Lazybones Quick Screen, you'll note that the overall assessment is mixed. The laundry industry is highly fragmented with lots of small mom-and-pop operators, with only 6 percent of the industry consisting of firms with 20 or more employees.[4] The three largest players, National Drycleaning Inc., Dry Clean USA, and Hangers America, have only 5.4 percent of the market share.[5] Lazybones is driven by the assumption that their professional process in handling college students' laundry is of value to potential franchisees. If so, then the company can secure franchisees and grow. However, considering that the overall industry isn't growing, it means that Lazybones's growth will come at the expense of competitors. In a highly fragmented industry, mom-and-pop competitors may not have the resources for a sustained fight with a larger player. The goal of the Quick Screen is to help you identify these critical assumptions before you spend considerable time and effort on a more thorough business planning process. The Quick Screen raises questions that you should work to answer as you proceed through the business planning process. As you view Lazybones's Quick Screen, what issues do you see? How would you advise Dan to manage these issues? We have created a Web site for your feedback on Lazybones at http://businessplansthatwork.groupsite.com. Input your thoughts on Lazybones and see how they compare with those of others who are reading this book. We have also created a networking site for you to share your questions and thoughts with other entrepreneurs who are early in their process. There is also an electronic Quick Screen at the Web site for you to use in evaluating your own ideas.

Ideally, would-be entrepreneurs have several concepts that they will screen before deciding which one to pursue. More often than not, however, entrepreneurs already have a strong vision for an opportunity that they are driven to pursue, even if the obstacles are many. We applaud both types of entrepreneurs. In the latter scenario, the Quick Screen will help you reshape the opportunity so that it is best positioned to succeed. There is no perfect deal. We find that entrepreneurs often think in terms of what

---

[4]IBISWorld, "IBISWorld Industry Report: Non Coin-Operated Laundromats and Dry Cleaners in the US," August 2009. http://www.ibisworld.com.ezproxy.babson.edu/industryus/default.aspx?indid=1730.

[5]Parent company: DCI Management Group Ltd.

can go right, whereas nonentrepreneurs immediately identify what can go wrong. The purpose of the business planning process is for you to identify what can go right, and then take steps in that direction.

Readers' Assessment and Exercising Your Entrepreneurship Quotient

Go back to the Lazybones Quick Screen. An assessment of Dan's Quick Screen exercises your entrepreneurship quotient (EQ). How would *you* rate each criterion? We recommend you use a colored pen to highlight your ranking versus ours. Do you see Dan's prospects differently than he does? If so, why? Do you think franchising is the best way to grow the business? What are the trade-offs in this approach? For your own idea, make copies of the Quick Screen and have team members separately evaluate and rank criteria. These separate rankings create the foundation for a team meeting that allows individuals to articulate their understanding of the opportunity. Debate the merits of different rating opinions. The result is a consolidated Quick Screen. Date that document and begin creating an opportunity audit trail. You might want to visit our Web site at http://businessplansthatwork.groupsite.com and use our electronic Quick Screen.

Many readers will disagree with Dan's assessment. Some will be critical and point out what can go wrong. Because there is no such thing as a perfect opportunity the flaws are the easiest place to start. That's okay but not sufficient to move an opportunity forward. For each problem offer a solution. At least map the activities you'll need to do to move the assessment closer to the "Go" position. For example, look at Quick Screen under the "Market- and Margin-Related Issues." Dan needs to decide what kind of training franchisees need. If you were to become a Lazybones franchisee, what kind of training would you want? How much do you think it would cost Dan to provide that training? What other types of support would you expect before you would buy a Lazybones franchise? Then go beyond the criticism and brainstorm about what might go *right*. How will good things move the Quick Screen evaluation and create value?

Venture Checkup and Thinking Big

The tenacious entrepreneur will shape her idea and logically move the Quick Screen ratings toward the "Go" conclusion. But you have to remember that while the Quick Screen exercise is important, it is purely hypothetical until you take action. The questions that the Quick Screen generates are its most important function. When you begin to take action, some of these questions will be answered, and new questions will arise. Therefore you gain the skills to constantly perform a venture checkup. Planning, action, and adjustments are integral to the entrepreneurial process. But before launch, the opportunity assessment and shaping process must eventually answer the scope and scale question. Is Dan thinking big enough?

Time and again the authors have observed the classic small business owner who, almost like a dairy farmer, is slaved and wedded to the business. Extremely long hours (70, 80, or even 100 hours a week), and rare vacations, are often the rule rather than the exception. And these hard-working owners rarely build equity, other than in the real estate they may own for the business. The implication is clear: one of the big differences between the growth- and equity-minded entrepreneur and the traditional small business owner is that the entrepreneur thinks *bigger*. Former venture capitalist Patricia Cloherty puts it this way: "It is critical to think big enough. If you want to start and build a company, you are going to end up exhausted. So you might as well think about creating a *big* company. At least you will end up exhausted and *rich*, not just exhausted!"

Pat has a wealth of experience as a venture capitalist and is past president of Patrioff & Company in New York City. She also served as the first female president of the National Venture Capital Association. In these capacities she has been a lead investor, board member, and creator of many highly successful high technology and biotechnology ventures, many of which were acquired or achieved an initial public offering (IPO). The constant action and shaping activity inherent in new venture creation should be done in the context of thinking big. The process of thinking big takes you on a journey always treading the fine line between high ambitions and being totally out of your mind. How do you know whether the idea you are chasing is just another rainbow or indeed has a bona fide pot of gold at the end? The truth is that you can never know which side of the line you are on—and can stay on—until you try and undertake the journey.

Once you are comfortable with the Quick Screen analysis, it is time to start thinking about the business plan. Before writing the different sections of the plan, it is useful to complete the Business Planning Guide.

The Business Planning Guide

The guide is based on the analytical framework described in the book and builds upon the Quick Screen. The Business Planning Guide will allow you to draw on data and analysis developed in the Opportunity Screening Exercises as you conduct your business planning.

As you proceed through the Business Planning Guide, remember that statements need to be supported with data whenever possible. Note also that it is sometimes easier to present data in graphic, visual form. In fact, visual presentation often more effectively communicates your vision. Include the source of all data, the methods and/or assumptions used, and the credentials of people doing research. If data on which a statement is based is available elsewhere in the plan, be sure to reference where it can be found.

Remember that the Business Planning Guide is just that—a guide. It is intended to be applicable to a wide range of product and service businesses. For any particular industry or market, certain critical issues are unique to that industry or market. In the chemical industry, for example, some special issues of significance currently exist, such as increasingly strict regulations at all levels of government concerning the use of chemical products and the operation of processes, diminishing viability of the high capital cost, special-purpose chemical processing plants serving a narrow market, and long delivery times of processing equipment. In the electronics industry, the special issues may be the future availability and price of new kinds of large-scale integrated circuits. Common sense should rule in applying the guide to your specific venture.

In the following exercise, we illustrate how Dan might complete this guide before he starts his business planning process. We have used broadly defined activities as you likely would in your first cut. As you start completing the tasks, you'll identify subtasks that complement the major tasks outlined. Put these into the schedule as you identify them. Although we expect that your scheduling of key activities will change, the discipline of going through the process keeps you focused on what needs to be done. If you start slipping on the deliverable due dates, it may be a signal that you were too aggressive in scheduling your dates, or it might signal other problems. For example, if you see that one team member is consistently slow on the deliverable, it may indicate that she is not a good person to retain because she might let you down once the business is launched. Just like the actual business plan, scheduling is a work in progress. Revisit your schedule regularly.

Exercise 1.2   *Business Planning Guide: Lazybones*

Name: Dan Hermann
Venture: Lazybones
Date: November 2010

Step 1: Segment Information into Key Sections

Establish priorities for each section, including individual responsibilities, and due dates for drafts and the final version. When you segment your information, it is vital to keep in mind that the plan needs to be logically integrated, and that information should be consistent. Note that, since the market opportunity section is the heart and soul of the plan, it may be the most difficult section to write, but it is best to assign it a high priority and to begin working there first. Remember to include such tasks as printing in the list.

Section or Task	Priority	Person(s) Responsible	Date to Begin	First Draft Due Date	Date Completed or Final Version Due Date
Laundry Industry Analysis and Seg- mentation	High	Dan	Immediately	December 1	December 15
Analysis of national competitors and franchisors	High	Joel	Immediately	December 1	December 15
Franchisor best prac- tices (across other industries).	High	Joel	November 15	December 8	December 22
Check with the International Franchise Associa- tion, Case Studies of McDonald's, Jiffy Lube, etc.	High	Dan	November 15	December 15	December 31
Document business format for the ideal Lazy- bones store	Moderate	Dan	November 15	December 8	December 22
University/location analysis (which areas are prime for franchise expansion?)	Moderate	Reg	Immediately	December 8	December 22
Create training man- ual and processes	Low	Reg	January 1	January 15	January 30
Evaluate current equipment and product suppliers against potential suppliers	Low	Reg	January 1	January 15	January 30

Exercise 1.2 *Business Planning Guide: Lazybones (continued)*

Step 2: List Tasks That Need to Be Completed

Devise an overall schedule for preparing the plan by assigning priority, persons responsible, and due dates to each task necessary to complete the plan. It is helpful to break larger items (fieldwork to gather customer and competitor intelligence, trade show visits, etc.) into small, more manageable components (such as phone calls required before a trip can be taken) and to include the components as a task. *Be as specific as possible.*

Task	Priority	Person Responsible	Date to Begin	Date of Completion
Industry	High	Dan	November 1	December 15
Customer	High	Dan	November 1	December 15
Competition	High	Joel	November 1	December 15
Company	Medium	Dan	December 1	December 22
Product	High	Reg	December 1	December 22
Marketing	High	Dan	December 15	January 7
Operations	Medium	Reg	December 15	January 7
Development	Medium	Joel	December 15	January 7
Team	Medium	Dan	December 15	January 7
Critical Risks	Medium	All	December 22	January 30
Offering	Medium	Joel	December 22	January 30
Financial Plan	Medium	Joel	December 22	January 30
Appendices	Medium	All	As needed	January 30

Step 3: Combine the List of Segments and the List of Tasks to Create a Calendar

In combining your lists, consider if anything has been omitted and whether you have been realistic as to what people can do, when they can do it, what needs to be done, and so forth. To create your calendar, place an X in the week when the task is to be started and an X in the week it is to be completed and then connect the Xs. When you have placed all tasks on the calendar, look carefully again for conflicts or lack of realism. In particular, evaluate whether team members are overscheduled.

Task								Week							
	1	2	3	4	5	6	7	8	9	10	11	12	13	14	15
Industry information	X	--	--	--	-- X										
Industry Segmentation	X	--	--	--	-- X										
Analyze Competition	X	--	--	--	-- X										
Customers	X	--	--	--	-- X										
Training Manual	X	--	--	--	-- -- X										
Franchise or Best Practices			X	--	-- -- X										

Task	1	2	3	4	5	6	7	8	9	10	11	12	13	14	15
								Week							
Location Analysis				X	-----------	-- X									
Company				X	-------	-- X									
Competition				X	------	-- X									
Product						X	--------	-- X							
Marketing						X	--------	-- X							
Operations						X	--------	-- X							
Development						X	--------	-- X							
Team							X	-----------------	-- X						
Critical Risks							X	-----------------	-- X						
Offering							X	-----------------	-- X						
Financial Plan															
Appendices						X	------------------------	-- X							

Step 4: A Framework to Develop and Write a Business Plan

While preparing your own plan, you will most likely want to consider sections in a different order from the one presented in this book. Also, when you integrate your sections into your final plan, you may choose to present material somewhat differently. The key is to make it *your* plan

Some Business Plan Basics: A Process

Business planning takes time and effort. You can expect to spend 200 hours creating your first draft. That is time well spent, not because it will insure that you raise the necessary capital, but because the process will help you answer the critical questions necessary to identify the opportunity and to reshape it so that it is a better opportunity. Remember, business planning is a means to an end, not the end result. The actual document will be obsolete the moment it comes out of the printer. Like all battle plans, it needs modification once the shooting starts.

There is a common misperception that a business plan is primarily used for raising capital. Although a good business plan assists in raising capital, the primary purpose of the process is to help entrepreneurs gain deep understanding of the opportunity they are envisioning. Business planning tests the feasibility of an idea. It is a dynamic process, like solving a jigsaw puzzle. Once you start filling in the blanks, you start seeing the real picture. Is it truly an opportunity? Many a would-be entrepreneur doggedly pursues ideas that are not opportunities, and the time invested in business planning would save thousands of dollars and hours spent on such "wild goose chases." For example, if a person makes $100,000 per year, spending 200 hours on business planning equates to a $10,000 investment in time spent ($50/hour times 200 hours). However, launching a flawed business concept can quickly accelerate into millions in losses. Most entrepreneurial ventures raise enough money to survive two years even if the business will ultimately fail. Assuming that the only expense is the time value of the lead entrepreneur, a two-year investment equates to $200,000, not to mention the lost opportunity cost and the likelihood that other employees were hired and paid and that other expenses were incurred. So do yourself a favor and spend the time and money up front in planning.

The business planning process not only can prevent an entrepreneur from pursuing a bad opportunity, it can also help entrepreneurs reshape their original vision into a better opportunity. The business planning process involves raising a number of critical questions and then seeking answers for those questions. Part of that question-answering process involves talking to target customers and gauging what is their "pain." These conversations with customers, as well as other trusted advisers, can assist in better targeting the features and needs that customers most want. This work prior to start-up saves untold effort and money that an entrepreneur might spend trying to reshape the product after the launch has occurred. This is not to say that new ventures don't adjust their offering based upon customer feedback, but the business planning process can anticipate some of these adjustments in advance of the initial launch.

Perhaps the greatest benefit of business planning is that it allows the entrepreneur to articulate the business opportunity to various stakeholders in the most effective manner. The planning provides the background so the entrepreneur can communicate the upside potential and attract equity investment. Business planning provides the validation needed to convince potential employees to leave their current job for the uncertain future of a new venture. It is also the instrument that can secure a strategic partner or key customer or key supplier. In short, business planning provides the entrepreneur the deep understanding needed to answer the critical questions that various stakeholders will ask, even if the stakeholders don't actually read the written plan. Completing a well-founded business plan gives the entrepreneur credibility in the eyes of various stakeholders. The process can sharpen thinking and strategies that define the risk and reward, and ultimately the odds for success. This book illustrates the most common business plan, but you should keep in mind that there are different types of business plans suitable for different purposes.

Types of Plans

A business plan can take a number of forms depending upon its purpose. The primary difference between business plan types is length and detail. If outside capital is needed, a business plan geared toward equity investors or debt providers is typically 25 to 40 pages long. This type of plan is also a good primer for new employees or for communicating the value of your enterprise to various stakeholders, such as a new supplier or customer. Entrepreneurs need to recognize that these stakeholders, especially professional equity investors such as venture capitalists and professional debt providers, will not read the entire plan from front to back. This being the case, the entrepreneur needs to produce the plan in a format that facilitates spot reading. This book investigates the major sections of business plans. Our general rule of thumb is that less is more. For instance, we've seen a number of plans receive venture funding that were closer to 25 pages rather than 40 pages.

A second type of business plan, the operational plan, is primarily for entrepreneurs and their team to guide the development, launch, and initial growth of the venture. There really is no length specification for this type of plan; however, it is common for these plans to exceed 80 pages. The basic organization format between the two types of plans is the same; however, the level of detail tends to be much greater in an operational plan. This effort is where the entrepreneur really gains the deep understanding so important in discerning how to build and run the business.

The last type of plan is called a dehydrated business plan. These plans are considerably shorter than the previous two; typically no more than 10 pages. The purpose of this plan is to provide an initial conception of the business; a more concise articulation of the people, the opportunity, and the finances required. As such, it can be used to test initial reaction to the entrepreneur's idea. It is a document that the entrepreneur can share with confidantes to receive feedback before investing significant time and effort on a longer business plan. This book illustrates the more traditional plan that can be used to raise capital and inform other stakeholders.

What type of plan will you write? Our guess is that you will use all three. In our experience, the dehydrated plan is good as an initial cut at what the business is. If you are working with a team, a dehydrated plan can be a road map to ensure that everyone has the same vision. Then you can delegate the writing of different portions of the plan to other team members. For instance, one person may write the marketing plan and another may write the development plan. Since each team member has the dehydrated plan as a guide, it will require less reconciliation when the entire plan is put together. We also find that dehydrated plans are good for sending to stakeholders in advance of meeting with them. Investors, for instance, are unlikely to read a 40-page plan unless they are really interested in the concept. Therefore, after you have completed the entire business planning process, come back and rewrite a spiffy dehydrated plan for external consumption. The dehydrated plan can be a tool to build interest from investors, customers, and suppliers.

The operational business plan is really a compilation of all the intelligence you and your team have gathered on the opportunity. It goes into a fine-grained level of detail on not only the opportunity but also the steps you'll take in launching the business. It has too much detail for external stakeholders, but it is invaluable to you.

Although we've detailed three types of written plans, most entrepreneurs and managers engage in a business planning process on a continuous basis. While you may not always document that planning in a written manner (maybe it is just a spreadsheet or a PowerPoint presentation), it is the process of planning that is important. With that in mind, the remainder of the book will walk you through the business planning process. Keep in mind that, although the chapters present the business plan sections sequentially, the process is more iterative. You'll write pieces of one section and then move to another section, before coming back and completing other parts of the plan. We cannot stress enough that the business planning process is dynamic and that the end result, a written plan, is obsolete the moment it comes off the printer. The business plan is a living document, one that you should revisit and revise often. Enjoy the process.

3 GETTING STARTED

Perhaps the hardest part of any business planning process is getting started. Compiling the data, shaping it into an articulate story, and producing the finished product can be daunting tasks. That being the case, it is best to use a stepwise approach to business planning. First, write a 25-word statement of your current vision. This provides a roadmap for you and others to follow as you start the planning process. Once the team agrees on the vision, expand it into a short summary of five to six pages. This expanded summary provides details and gives you momentum to start attacking major sections of the plan.

Although all of the sections interact and influence every other section, it is often easiest for entrepreneurs to write the product/service description first. This is usually the most concrete component of the entrepreneur's vision. Keep in mind, however, that business planning isn't a purely sequential process. You will be filling in different parts of the plan simultaneously or in whatever order is dictated by new information or makes the most sense in your mind. Finally, after completing a first draft of all the major sections, it is time to come back and rewrite a shorter, more concise executive summary (one to two pages). Not too surprisingly, the executive summary will be quite different from the original summary because of all the learning and reshaping that the business planning process facilitates.

As you begin this task, perhaps the most important thing to consider is that the business plan is a "living document." Although your first draft will be polished, most business plans are obsolete the day they come out of the printer. Thus entrepreneurs are continuously updating and revising their business plan since the entire context is constantly changing. Can anyone tell you who all your competitors are *today*, let alone in a *month*? Again, the importance of the business plan isn't the final product, but the learning that is gleaned from going through the process and the habit of reshaping your plan. Through each iteration, you will learn more; for example, you will identify more competitors in the next iteration than in the first. The business plan is the novel of your vision. It articulates what you see in your mind, as well as crystallizing that vision for you and your team. It also provides a history, a photo album if you will, of the birth, growth, and maturation of your business. Each major revision should be kept and filed and occasionally looked back upon for the lessons you have learned. Although daunting, we find writing a business plan exciting and creative, especially if you are working on it with a founding team. Whether it is over a glass of wine, mug of beer, or cup of coffee, talking about your business concept with your founding team is invigorating, and the business plan is a critical outcome of these discussions. So now, let us dig in and examine how to develop and write effective business plans.

The Story Model: A Plan for Whom?

One of the major goals for business plans is to attract and convince various stakeholders of the potential of your business. Therefore, you have to keep in mind how these stakeholders will interpret your plan: who is the plan for?—you, potential team members, a brain trust adviser, investors, customers? The guiding principal is that you are writing a story. All good stories have a plot line, a unifying thread that ties the characters and events together. If you think about the most successful businesses in America, they all have well publicized plot lines, or more appropriately, taglines. When you hear these taglines, you immediately connect them to the business. For example, when you hear "absolutely, positively has to be there overnight," most people think of Federal Express and package delivery. Similarly, "Just do it" is intricately linked to Nike and the image of athletic excellence (Fig. 3.1). A tagline is a sentence, or even a fragment of a sentence, that summarizes the pure essence of your business. It is the plot line that every sentence, paragraph, page, and diagram within your business plan should correlate to. One useful tip that we share with every entrepreneur we work with is to put that tagline in a footer that runs on the bottom of every page. Most word processing packages, such as Microsoft Word, enable you to insert a footer that you can see as you type. As you are writing, if the section doesn't build on, explain, or otherwise directly relate to the tagline, it most likely isn't a necessary com-

Figure 3.1 *Taglines*

Facebook	*Giving people the power to share and make the world more open and connected.*
Twitter	*Discover what's happening right now, anywhere in the world.*
Google	*Search, ads & apps*
Nike	*Just Do It*
Federal Express	*When it absolutely, positively has to be there overnight.*
McDonald's	*We love to see you smile.*
Cisco Systems	*Empowering the Internet generation.*
Microsoft	*Where do you want to go today?*

ponent of the business plan. Rigorous adherence to the tagline facilitates writing a concise business plan.

The key to the story model is capturing the reader's attention. The tagline is the foundation, but in writing the plan, you want to create a number of visual catch-points. Too many business plans are text laden, dense manifestos. Only the most diligent reader will wade through all that text to find the nuggets of value. Help the reader by highlighting different key points throughout the plan. How do you create these catch-points? Some effective techniques include extensive use of headings and subheadings, strategically placed bullet point lists, diagrams, charts, and the use of sidebars.[1] The point is to make the document not only content rich but visually attractive and easy for the reader to identify highlights.

Now, let's look at the major sections of the plan (Fig. 3.2). Keep in mind that, although there are some variations, most plans have these components. It is important to keep your plan as close to this format as possible because many stakeholders are used to the format and it facilitates spot reading. So if you are seeking venture capital for instance, you want to facilitate quick perusal, because it has been found that venture capitalists often spend as little as five minutes on a plan before rejecting it or putting it aside for further attention. A venture capitalist who becomes frustrated with an unfamiliar format is more likely to reject it rather than try to pull out the pertinent information. Although other types of investors,

---

[1]Running sidebar is a visual device that is positioned down the right hand side of the page that periodically highlights some of the key points in the plan. Don't overload the sidebar, but one or two items per page can draw attention to highlights that maintain reader interest.

Figure 3.2 *Business Plan Outline*

I.   Cover
II.   Executive summary
III.   Table of contents
IV.   Industry, customer, and competitor analysis
V.   Company and product description
VI.   Marketing plan
VII.   Operations plan
VIII.   Development plan
IX.   Team
X.   Critical risks
XI.   Offering
XII.   Financial plan
XIII.   Appendices

such as friends, family, and angels might be more patient than a venture capitalist, keeping the venture capitalist in mind will help you write a concise, effective plan that is more likely to impress all stakeholders.

Cover Page

The cover of the plan should include the following information: company name, tagline, contact person and address, phone, fax, e-mail, date, disclaimer, and copy number. Most of the information is self-explanatory, but a few things should be pointed out. First, the contact person for a new venture should be the president or some other founding team member. We have seen some business plans that failed to have the contact person's name, phone, and e-mail address on the cover. Imagine the frustration of an excited potential investor who can't find out how to contact the entrepreneur to gain more information. More often than not, that plan will end up in the rejected pile. Second, business plans should have a disclaimer along these lines:

> This business plan has been submitted on a confidential basis solely to selected, highly qualified investors. The recipient should not reproduce this plan, nor distribute it to others without permission. Please return this copy if you do not wish to invest in the company.

Controlling distribution is particularly important when seeking investment, especially if you do not want to violate Regulation D of the U.S. Securities and Exchange Commission (SEC), which specifies how many unaccredited investors can invest in your firm.[2]

The cover should also have a line stating the copy number. So, for example, you will often see on the bottom right portion of the cover a line that says, "Copy 1 of 5 copies." Entrepreneurs should keep a log of who has copies so that they can control for unexpected distribution. Finally, the cover should be eye-catching. If you have a product or prototype, a picture of it can draw the reader in. Likewise, a catchy tagline draws attention and encourages the reader to look further. Let's take a look at the Lazybones' cover page.

---

[2]Going into detail on SEC regulations is beyond the scope of this book, and if in doubt you should check with your lawyer; however, here are a few of the basics. If your total financing need (private placement) is under $1 million, there aren't any federal restrictions, other than antifraud rules. If it is over $1 million, you can only have 35 unaccredited investors. In order for an individual to qualify as an accredited investor, he or she must accomplish at least one of the following:

1. Earn an individual income of more than $200,000 per year, or a joint income of $300,000, in each of the last two years and expect to reasonably maintain the same level of income
2. Have a net worth exceeding $1 million, either individually or jointly with his or her spouse
3. Be a general partner, executive officer, director, or a related combination thereof for the issuer of a security being offered

These investors are considered to be fully functional without all the restrictions of the SEC.

Lazybones Cover Page

Laundry like your Mom does it

Tagline gives you a sense of the business.

Business plan date allows you to easily track the version of the plan. Remember, business planning is an ongoing process, so you'll likely have multiple versions.

Business Plan
April 2009

Dan Hermann
dhermann1@babson.edu
(617) 966-5299 cell
Joel Pedlikin
joelped@gmail.com
(617) 633-4919 cell

Contact person and information is easy to find.

Catalog who you've sent each plan to. This will help you keep track of who has it, along with what version they have. It also provides a reminder of the folks you should communicate with to give updates and judge their investment readiness.

Copy____ of____

-CONFIDENTIAL-

The components of this business plan have been submitted on a confidential basis. Neither can it be reproduced, stored, or copied in any form. By accepting delivery of this plan the recipient agrees to return this copy of the plan. Do not copy, fax, reproduce, or distribute without permission.

While it is impossible to prevent unwanted distribution of your plan, the confidentiality statement at least makes recipients aware that they should not pass the plan along to someone else without permission.

Executive Summary

This section is the most important part of the business plan. If you don't capture readers' attention in the executive summary, it is unlikely that they will read any other parts of the plan or contact you for more information. In a recent interview of 10 venture capital veterans, all of them said they discarded a plan after reading the executive summary if it didn't present a compelling story. Therefore, you want to hit them with the most compelling aspects of your business opportunity right up front. *Hook the reader.* That means having the first sentence or paragraph highlight the potential of the opportunity. We have read too many plans that start with "Company XYZ, incorporated in the state of Delaware, will develop and sell widgets." Ho-hum. That doesn't excite us, but the first sentences could instead state the following: "The current market for widgets is $50 million, growing at an annual rate of 20 percent. Moreover, the emergence of the Internet 2.0 is likely to accelerate this market's growth. Company XYZ is positioned to capture this wave with its proprietary technology; the secret formula VOOM. The founding team has over 60 years of experience in starting and building three companies in a related technology and market area. Two of these businesses were sold, and the third is a public company with sales over $100 million." This creates the right tone. It tells us that the potential opportunity is huge and that company XYZ has some competitive advantage that enables it to become a big player in this market. Moreover, the strength of the founding team and its track record would be attractive to investors. We don't really care, at this point, whether the business is incorporated or that it is a Delaware corporation (aren't they all?).

Common subsections within the executive summary include the following: Description of Opportunity, Business Concept, Industry Overview, Target Market, Competitive Advantage, Business Model and Compelling Economics, Team, and Offering. Remember that, since this is an executive summary, all these components are covered in the body of the plan. As such, we will explore them in detail as we progress through the remainder of the book.

Because the executive summary is the most important part of the finished plan, it should be written after you have gained your deep learning by going through all the other sections.[3] The summary should be one to three pages, although we prefer executive summaries to be no more than two pages.

---

[3]Don't confuse the executive summary included in the plan with the expanded executive summary that we suggested you write as the very first step of the business plan process. Again, the two summaries are likely to be significantly different as the later summary incorporates all the deep learning that you have gained throughout the process.

Lazybones Executive Summary

Hook: Notice how the executive summary captures the essence of the customer (parent as payer and student as user). This opening quote validates the need for this type of service, especially since it is pulled from an outside source.

Business description.

Notice the use of headings to help guide the reader.

Notice how they redefine their marketplace away from laundry services (which is very mature with flat growth) to a niche of personal services for college students (which has room for growth). This is a more compelling story.

Suggests an attractive market.

While at first glance, this would seem to be a negative, the audience for this story is potential franchisees. Dan is communicating that you don't need extensive experience in laundry or services to succeed in this business.

Executive Summary

"There is now such intense competition between universities that … 'a luxury arms race' has broken out to bag America's most affluent students … and the rich cannot bear to see their little darlings suffer the indignities of, well, college life.[4]"

Fortunately for Lazybones, laundry is one of the things parents prefer to provide for their children, and as a result we have been highly profitable providing both laundry and storage services to college students for 15 years.
Net profit margins around 20 percent are not, however, the only attribute that has Lazybones poised for aggressive growth.

Opportunity

Lazybones operates at the intersection of two exploding segments in two large, mature industries: personal services for wealthy college students, and personal services franchising.

Personal services franchising generated over $90 billion in revenue in 2005 and grew on average 11 percent per year since 2001.[5]

Each of its four current locations (Madison, Wisconsin; Syracuse, New York; Boulder, Colorado; and Boston, Massachusetts) is run by inexperienced managers with hourly staffs.

---

[4]Wapshott, N. *New Statesman Magazine*, September 2008. http://www.newstatesman.com/society/2008/09/university-america-student
[5]Price Waterhouse Coopers, "The Economic Impact of Franchise Businesses volume II: Results for 2005," January 31, 2008. http://www.franchise.org/uploadedFiles/Franchisors/Other_Content/economic_impact_documents/EconImpact_Vol2_HiLights.pdf

This is accomplished with centralized Web technologies, support from experienced executives/owners, and proprietary business systems that have been being developed, tested, and tweaked for 15 years. Thanks to the current recession, hundreds of thousands of highly motivated, high-energy individuals who would thrive running a Lazybones franchise are seeking the job security that running their own business could provide—and franchising is the most common and least risky path to running their own business. Lazybones will offer a lucrative, low-initial-investment opportunity to individuals eager to own their piece of the American Dream. By opening four more company stores while aggressively selling franchises, the company will expand across the United States, growing its revenues sixfold over five years while increasing its already high profit margins.

Company Performance

Lazybones's four locations generated 2008 revenues of ~$1.2 million: laundry and dry cleaning services accounted for roughly two-thirds and summer storage and shipping the remaining third.

Receiving advance payments from parents for a semesters' services keeps the Lazybones cash flows and balance sheet clean and strong.

Competition exists mainly in the form of small localized businesses.

A few of these companies offer competing services on multiple campuses but none at more than 10 locations. Over a decade of operations at the Madison, Wisconsin, and Syracuse, New York, locations has enabled Lazybones to develop competitive advantages that allow the company to outpace these competitors. All of this experience has also provided extensive information about what works in the business model, so that operations systems and manuals already exist in easily transferable forms. All of these factors have prepared Lazybones for rapid expansion into the more than 1,600 viable campus locations.

Team

Joel Pedlikin will join current founding partner Dan Hermann and founding partner Reg Mathelier to round out the company's leadership team. Joel's 10 years of executive experience with

This shows that Lazybones has strong systems to support potential franchisees. This underscores the company's ability to get to a national scale.

This begins to set milestone growth objectives that will manage investor relations and create a pathway to increased valuation for multiple rounds of investment.

This establishes multiple revenue streams.

Strong cash flow characteristics are appealing to investors, especially angels.

Identifies the fragmented nature of the industry. Mostly mom-and-pop stores, which suggests that a professionalized operation should have a competitive advantage.

Identifies national market potential across the country.

Since Lazybones has a 15-year operating history, the team section focuses on the newest team member. What is missing is someone with franchising experience. While Dan and Reg can operate a small chain, it isn't necessarily clear that they can manage as a franchisor.

companies in the $12 million to $50 million range, as well as his two engineering degrees from Brown and Caltech infuse much needed experience and energy to the company's founders at this critical growth stage.

Financial Snapshot: *Five-Year Income Statement*

	Year 1	Year 2	Year 3	Year 4	Year 5
Revenue					
Total Number of owned Stores	8	8	8	8	8
Total Number of franchises	0	5	15	35	60
Owned Store Contribution	$2,033,177	$2,971,381	$4,089,183	$5,225,870	$6,125,353
Franchise Contribution	$0	$206,905	$485,348	$1,100,699	$1,767,146
Total Revenue	$2,033,177	$3,178,286	$4,574,531	$6,326,569	$7,891,599
Total COGS*	$872,835	$1,309,072	$1,296,739	$1,585,962	$1,747,125
Gross Profit	$1,160,342	$1,869,213	$3,277,792	$4,740,607	$6,144,474
Gross Profit %	57%	59%	72%	75%	78%
Expenses					
Owned Store SG&A**	$1,358,133	$1,371,987	$1,469,757	$1,558,780	$1,624,546
Corporate SG&A	$328,314	$344,730	$664,870	$728,201	$976,651
Taxes and Interest Expenses	$70,876	$143,164	$521,722	$1,027,290	$1,432,920
Total Expenses	$1,757,323	$1,859,881	$2,656,350	$3,314,272	$4,034,117
Net Ordinary Income	−$596,981	$95,333	$621,466	$1,426,336	$2,110,357
Net Profit Margin	−29%	0%	14%	23%	26%

* COGS = cost of goods sold
** SG&A = selling, general and administrative expenses

This abbreviated income statement gives a sense of the five-year plan and potential for Lazybones. However, the executive summary seems to be missing a discussion of how the team plans to finance the $600,000 loss in year 1. Will this come from current cash flow or do they need outside investment?

Table of Contents

Continuing the theme of making the document easy to read, a detailed table of contents is critical. Many investors, for example, prefer to spot read business plans versus reading them from front to back. Help such readers easily find the information they want. The table of contents should include major sections, subsections, exhibits, and appendices. The table provides the reader a roadmap to your plan. Note that the table of contents is customized to the specific business so that it doesn't perfectly correlate to the business plan outline presented earlier (see Fig. 3.2). Nonetheless, a look at the Lazybones plan shows that it includes most of the elements highlighted in the business outline and that the order of information is basically the same as well.

The first three sections directly relate to the due diligence prescribed in the Timmons Model. The Market Analysis and Competition sections translate your opportunity analysis described in Chapter 1. The Company description section is the unique way in which you will mine that opportunity. The Team section is often later in the plan to provide an exclamation point. Up until that point, you have identified the opportunity, your company's solution, and how you will execute the plan. The Team section illustrates that you have the horsepower to succeed.

Lazybones Table of Contents

Major headings are denoted as 1, 2, 3 and subheads are denoted as 1.1, 1.2, etc.

Notice how they highlight exhibits. Telling your story in "pictures" conveys lots of information quickly and concisely.

Chapter Summary

The most important part of any business plan is the executive summary. Although you should write the final version that is included in the business plan after all the other sections are completed, drafting an extended version prior to digging into the other sections can help you clarify your vision. You can share this early draft with fellow team members to ensure that you are all on the same page. The final version of the executive summary is the most important part of the plan. It not only acts as a hook to entice investors and other stakeholders to take a closer look, it is your concise articulation of the opportunity. We find that entrepreneurs who can clearly articulate their opportunity are more successful in convincing others to join or invest. The remaining chapters examine in detail the different sections of the plan.

4

INDUSTRY: ZOOM LENS ON OPPORTUNITY

The goal of this section is to illustrate the opportunity, the size of the market, and why there is a significant market to capture. Figure 4.1 provides the typical structure for this section. We start with the industry definition. What is the broader industry in which your venture will participate? We try to be expansive about our industry definition to keep clear the vastness of the opportunity, even if we will attack a specific niche. For instance, Lazybones operates in the laundry industry. We can use the opportunity component from the Timmons Model described in Chapter 1 to articulate the opportunity. Detail the industry size, growth rate, and major industry players (sometimes called market structure). Talk about the nature of the industry. Is market demand increasing with no dominant player? We call this an *emerging market*. Are smaller players failing or being acquired by a few dominant players? We call that a consolidating market. Are there clear market leaders who are stable and dominant with slow growth? This is a mature market. Next, we suggest you talk about major trends that are occurring in the industry. For example, Lazybones points out that while dry cleaning, a major segment in the laundry industry is declining, other segments focused on niche customers such as college students are poised for growth. The plan also highlights that franchising is experiencing rapid growth even during the recession. Explaining the pertinent trends bolsters the opportunity and suggests what white space there might be within the industry. Market growths, channels of distribution, and new technologies or innovations are a few trends that need to be examined closely. Your assessment of industry trends is an important part of the articulation of your vision.

Figure 4.1 *Industry Section*

I. **Industry definition**
   A. Size
   B. Growth
   C. Major players
   D. Trends
II. **Segments**
   A. Define
   B. Your segment
   C. Size, growth, major players
   D. Trends

The next step is to define the segments within the industry. For example, Lazybones segments the laundry industry into dry cleaning, commercial laundries, coin-operated laundries, and so forth. Then you need to define your niche in similar terms as you defined the industry. Specifically, detail the size, growth, major players, and trends that impact the environment you will enter. Interestingly, Lazybones may be a disruptive business model because it crafts a new service model and channel of distribution, but that discussion will come later.

A common error in writing this section is to focus on your own company. It's premature to talk about your company without first setting the scene. Instead, use dispassionate, arms-length analysis of the industry with the goal of highlighting a space or gap that is underserved. You are creating the stage to introduce your company a bit later in the plan. Remember, most people will have read the executive summary so they know what your concept is and can use that reference to assess whether they believe your description of the competitive environment.

As the entrepreneur, you should keep in mind how people will read the plan. Every statement and statistic you cite adds credibility and reinforces your story, but it also triggers areas that readers will want to investigate. As we read plans, for instance, we think about ways to validate entrepreneurs' claims. In other words, we start constructing a due diligence schedule. That means identifying key assumptions, such as the Lazybones assertion that the college laundry sector is prime for franchising when the laundry industry as a whole has relatively few franchisors. To validate, we might contact our brain trust members (people with industry expertise who the entrepreneur has built a relationship with and who can gauge whether Dan's scenario makes sense), talk to customers, distributors, and even competitors. Notice that the types of actions that investors or other stakeholders might take mirror actions that you as an entrepreneur should take before the investor ever reads your plan. Thus entrepreneurs can often guide stakeholders in their due diligence by connecting them with customers and others who the entrepreneur has already spoken with. Let's take a look at the Lazybones industry section.

Lazybones Industry Analysis Section

SECTION 1: INDUSTRY

Lazybones operates in the non-coin-operated laundry industry but will compete in the franchise industry and operate on university college campuses. To successfully grasp the Lazybones opportunity we must first understand each of these industries.

> Note how they are laying out the context in which they compete. It isn't solely confined to the laundry industry, but they will also compete for franchisees and for college student services. It should be noted, however, that franchising isn't technically an industry, it is a distribution channel.

1.1 Non-Coin-Operated Laundry and Dry Cleaning Industry

The non-coin-operated laundry and dry cleaning industry is a $10 billion industry annually, of which laundry services make up about 23 percent (Exhibit 1.1).

Exhibit 1.1 *Industry Segments*[1]

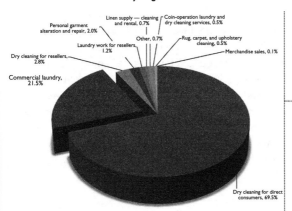

> A picture is worth a thousand words. This pie chart captures the entire industry. Note how Lazybones separates the pie piece (commercial laundry) where it competes from the overall industry. By showing the entire chart the company leaves room for future opportunities in adjacent or related markets. Also note that all stats and facts are footnoted, which adds validity to the analysis.

[1]IBISWorld, "IBISWorld Industry Report: Non Coin-Operated Laundromats and Dry Cleaners in the US," October 14 2008. http://www.ibisworld.com.ezproxy.babson.edu/industryus/default.aspx?indid=1730.

> Lazybones further subdivides its segment to focus on noncommercial customers. Later in this section, they will drill down even further and talk about the college student user. The key when talking about your industry is to start with the overall industry and then funnel down to the segment where you will compete.

Our direct market is within the roughly 50 percent of this segment that caters to noncommercial customers, meaning the overall laundry market size relevant to Lazybones is about $1 billion. On whole the industry is mature, with revenues and growth remaining relatively steady for the last five years (Exhibit 1.2).

Exhibit 1.2 *Industry Revenue and Revenue Growth, 2004–2008[2]*

> Part of the Lazybones story is that the industry can be consolidated through professionalizing the services. A franchise would bring consistency and brand recognition to the customers. Again, the assumption is that the customer will prefer a recognizable and arguably predictable service represented by the Lazybones brand.

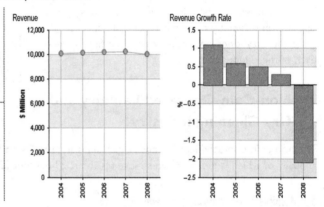

Concentration in this industry is extremely low. It is still largely composed of owner-operated family businesses with less than 6 percent of this market accounted for by larger companies (Exhibit 1.3). Revenue growth has been in slight (3 percent) decline industrywide (see Exhibit 1.2) over the past five years due to a reduction in dry cleaning revenues. Dry cleaners have been "affected by a decreased need for their services, due to trends towards wash-and-wear fabrics and improved laundry powders and fluids for use in the home."[3]

> Notice that throughout the plan, Lazybones uses secondary sources to size and quantify the nature of the opportunity. Footnoting these sources adds credibility to your story.

---

[2]Ibid.
[3]Ibid.

Exhibit 1.3 *Employment Size by Establishment, 2005*[4]

> This chart bolsters the Lazybones argument that the market is ripe for consolidation by an innovative new player with a logical national expansion plan.

Employee Size	Units Establishments	Percent Total
1–4	15,880	58.4
5–9	5,907	21.7
10–19	3,707	13.6
20–49	1,469	5.4
50–99	175	0.6
100–250	54	0.2
250–499	7	0.0
500–999	2	0.0
1000+	1	0.0
Total	27,196	

Source: US Census—County Business Patterns.
Note: Released June 2007. Information relates to employer establishments only.

There are only a few big companies in this space, and fewer still are franchises. Most notable among them are Dry Clean USA and Cool Clean Technologies, which operates franchises under the name Hangers America, LLC (Exhibit 1.4).

Exhibit 1.4 *Major Players*[5]

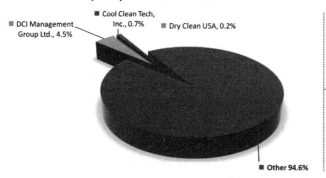

■ DCI Management Group Ltd., 4.5%
■ Cool Clean Tech, Inc., 0.7%
■ Dry Clean USA, 0.2%
■ Other 94.6%

> Notice how Lazybones highlights trends that suggest its focus on laundry is in a growth phase even though the industry as a whole is in slow decline.

[4]Ibid.
[5]Ibid.

Trends

The industry on the whole is in a slow, long-term decline, but this is driven by the dry cleaning segment. According to IBISWorld's 2008 industry report, laundry services are in a growth stage resulting from rapid growth in the tourism, hospitality, and retail fashion trades. The report identifies these key industry success factors:

- The ability to quickly adopt new technology
- The ability to accommodate environmental requirements
- Proximity to key markets
- Access to niche markets (so as to move away from general price-based competition),

1.2 Franchising Overview

> Lazybones is bringing together laundry and franchising so it needs to talk about the franchising as well.

The U.S. franchise industry is huge. In 2005, there were 909,253 franchised establishments that produced output worth $880.9 billion and provided 11.0 million jobs.[6] Franchised businesses accounted for 4.4 percent of *all* public sector output in that year. It is also a growing industry.

Between 2001 and 2005 output generated by franchised businesses grew at an average annual rate of 9 percent.

There are a wide variety of business format franchise[7] segments within the industry. A typical segmentation, along with the revenues per segment in 2005, is shown in Exhibit 1.5. Lazybones fits into the fastest-growing segment,

> Again, the growth in this industry supports the Lazybones story that this is an attractive opportunity.

personal services, which represents about 10 percent of the franchise market on the whole ($96 billion in 2005). This segment grew 53.8 percent in the four years between 2001 and 2005.

---

[6]Ibid.

[7]The industry is typically divided into business format and traditional franchisers. Traditional franchisers, like gas stations, allow franchisees to resell or distribute a product along with its registered trademark. Business format franchisers, like fast-food restaurants, offer their franchisees a format for running the business and operational support. Business format franchisers have become by far the dominant variety, representing 76 percent of total franchise revenues in 2007.

Exhibit 1.5   *Franchising by Segment, 2007*[8]

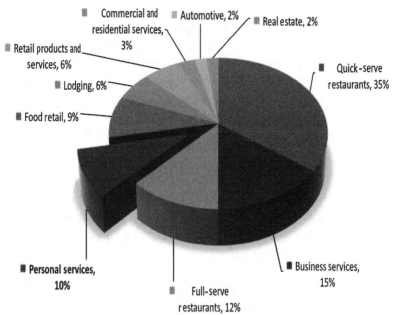

- Commercial and residential services, 3%
- Automotive, 2%
- Real estate, 2%
- Retail products and services, 6%
- Lodging, 6%
- Food retail, 9%
- Quick-serve restaurants, 35%
- Personal services, 10%
- Full-serve restaurants, 12%
- Business services, 15%

Exhibit 1.6   *Personal Services Segment 2001–2005*[9]

	2001	2005	% Change	Avg % Growth Rate
Jobs	753,793	937,853	24.40	5.60
Payroll	$26.2 billion	$37.1 billion	41.40	9.10
Output	$62.5 billion	$96.1 billion	53.80	11.40
Establishments	54,826	76,824	40.10	8.80

[8]Price Waterhouse Coopers, "The Economic Impact of Franchise Businesses Volume II: Results for 2005," January 31, 2008. http://www.franchise.org/uploadedFiles/Franchisors/Other_Content/economic_impact_documents/EconImpact_Vol2_HiLights.pdf.
[9]Ibid.

This section provides the basic parameters of the franchising industry. It should be noted that franchises are sometimes categorized in two ways; business format franchises like McDonald's and Jiffy Lube and product franchises like Whirlpool Appliances. The Lazybones plan describes a business format franchise.

Business format franchisers are typically paid by franchisees in three ways:

• Franchise fees, a fixed sum paid to the franchiser at start-up. These can vary from $10,000 to $100,000. The industry average in 2001 was $22,000 ($26,000 if adjusted for inflation to 2008). The average for the personal services segment was $18,600 ($22,150 if adjusted for inflation to 2008).[10] Note that this is strictly the fee paid to the franchiser. The total costs for starting a franchise are typically much higher (Exhibit 1.7).

• Royalty rates, a fixed percentage of a franchisee's revenue paid to the franchiser on a monthly or quarterly basis. These can vary from 1 to 15 percent. The industry average in 2001 was 5.2 percent. The average for the personal services segment was 5.1 percent[11] (Exhibit 1.8).

• Advertising fees. Franchisees contribute a fixed percentage of their revenue into a central advertising fund, which is used by the franchiser to run a national advertising campaign.

Exhibit 1.7 *Franchising Fees, 2001[12]*

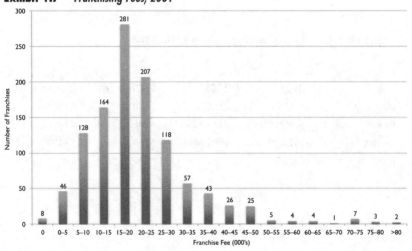

[10]Roger Blair and Franchine LaFontaine, The Economics of Franchising, Cambridge University Press, 2005, 57–71.
[11]Ibid.
[12]Ibid.

Exhibit 1.8 *Franchising Royalty Rate (Percent of Revenue), 2001*[13]

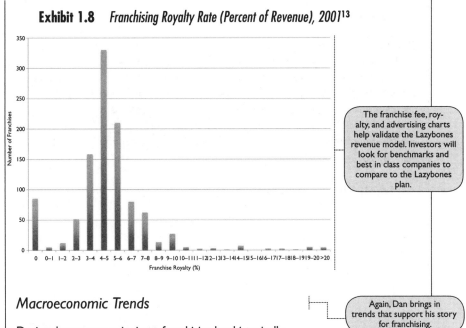

The franchise fee, royalty, and advertising charts help validate the Lazybones revenue model. Investors will look for benchmarks and best in class companies to compare to the Lazybones plan.

Macroeconomic Trends

Again, Dan brings in trends that support his story for franchising.

During down economic times, franchising has historically outperformed independent businesses. A major reason is job security. November 2008 alone saw the layoffs of over 91,000 U.S. workers,[14] and it doesn't take long for unemployed people to seek alternatives. Workers who lose their jobs are especially eager for job security, and running one's own business frequently looks like a more secure option after one has been laid off. For those who have not run a business before, franchising is a particularly appealing route.

> What's more indicative of the resilience of the industry is the fact that the economic output due to franchising grew by more than 40% [between 2001 and 2005], while all other businesses increased by only 26%. Employment in franchising grew by more than 12% compared to the 3% of other businesses. These growth rates have proven, beyond anecdotal evidence, that franchising is counter-cyclical to an underperforming economy.
>
> —Matthew Shay, President, International Franchising Association.[15]

---

[13]Ibid.
[14]Forbes.com layoff tracker.
[15]"Franchising Weathers Economic Challenges," Franchising World, May 2008. Page 8.

1.3 University/College Industry

The Lazybones market is college students. Therefore, our success depends on a solid understanding of the size and trends of the university/college industry. We will touch on the industry's revenues, but our main focus is on the numbers of students (potential customers) in this market and, more importantly, the numbers, sizes, and tuition costs of potential campus locations for Lazybones.

The university/college industry hit $425 billion in 2008. It is a mature industry in a steady growth phase with revenues predicted to exceed the $500 billion mark by 2012 (Exhibit 1. 9).

Exhibit 1.9 *University College Industry Revenue and Growth, 1997–2013 (projected beyond 2008)[16]*

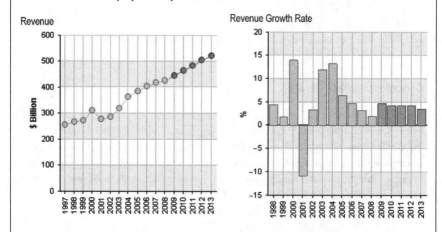

According to the National Center for Education Statistics, there were an estimated 11.2 million college students in the fall of 2007 and 2,629 four-year degree-granting institutions in the United States. Of these, 1,633 had campuses of over 2,500 students (Exhibit 1.10).

[16]IBISWorld, "IBISWorld Industry Report: University Colleges in the U.S." September 22, 2008. http://www.ibisworld.com.ezproxy.babson.edu/industryus/default. aspx?indid=1529.

Exhibit 1.10 *University Colleges by Enrollment and Type, 2007*[17]

Type and control of institution	Total	<499	999	Enrollment Size 500– 2,499	1,000– 4,999	2,500– 9,999	5,000– 19,999	10,000– 29,999	20,000– >30,000
Total number of institutions	4,253	1,099	605	916	657	484	311	126	55
Public	1,675	66	91	328	382	384	263	113	48
Private	2,678	1,033	514	588	275	100	13	13	7
Total enrollment of institutions	17,487,475	264,916	435,812	1,521,898	2,347,306	3,397,028	4,292,326	3,057,138	2,171,051

Tuitions at these institutions cover a wide range, with approximately 600 charging over $18,000 a year (Exhibit 1.11).

Exhibit 1.11 *University College Tuitions, 2008*[18]

U.S. Four-Year Colleges

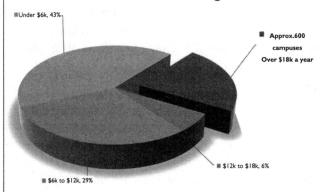

■ Under $6k, 43%

■ Approx.600 campuses Over $18k a year

■ $12k to $18k, 6%

■ $6k to $12k, 29%

> This chart highlights the core marketplace for Lazybones. The 600 campuses where tuition exceeds $18,000/ year. Note, there are some trends that pose risks, such as the impact of online learning and how that might impact the number of students living on campus.

1,600 campuses with enrollment over 2,500 students

[17]U.S. Dept. of Education, National Center for Education Statistics, 2005 Integrated Post-secondary Education Data System, Spring 2006. http://nces.ed.gov/.

[18]IBISWorld, "IBISWorld Industry Report: University Colleges in the U.S." September 22, 2008. http://www.ibisworld.com.ezproxy.babson.edu/industryus/default.aspx?indid=1529

CUSTOMER

The defined market space you plan to enter and the target customer in that space needs to be examined in detail. The entrepreneur needs to define who the customer is by using demographic, psychographic, and behavioral information. The better the entrepreneur can define her customer, the more apt she is to deliver a product that the customer truly wants. Venture capitalists often say that the most impressive entrepreneur is the one who comes into their office and not only identifies who the customer is in terms of demographics, psychographics, and behavior but can also name who that customer is by address, phone number, and e-mail address. When you understand who your customer is, you can assess what compels them to buy, how your company can sell to them (direct sales, retail, Internet, direct mail, etc.), how much it is going to cost to acquire and retain that customer, and so forth. A schedule inserted into the text that describes customers based on the basic parameters can be very powerful. It communicates a lot of data quickly.

The key to understanding your customers is to really get to know them. The best means of doing so, prior to launch, is to talk to them and observe their behavior. Many would-be entrepreneurs fail to talk to their customers. They assume that, since they would be interested in their own product, so would others. This is often a fatal assumption. We encourage you to have informal conversations with your customers. If at all possible, observe them doing the activity or work that your product or service would make better, easier, or more cost-effective. Taking such action will help you modify your offering so that you can better meet customer expectations. Lazybones is at an advantage since they have been selling to college students for 15 years, and the current plan is to expand to other campuses. You can see that Dan and his team really understand the customer. They have identified the user (the student) and the payer (the parent). As you read the customer section of the plan, you can also see that they understand what hurdles they have to overcome to get students to use their service (fear that clothes will be lost or damaged). The fact that he has worked with his customers and learned what customer profile best matches his likely users lessens the perceived risk that the franchising expansion won't succeed.

Talking to your customer is invaluable, but you can also gain insight by talking to others who have knowledge of your customer. Talk to your potential suppliers, competition,[19] and other people and companies involved in the market space. Going to a trade show is invaluable. In such venues, people gather to share information so your competitors might be more likely to discuss what they perceive as the customer's needs. Dan and his team, for example, regularly attend franchising trade shows, such as the International Franchise Expo, to learn about both potential customers (franchisees who might want to buy a Lazybones franchise) and competitors (other service franchises). The key to truly understanding your customer is to do primary research. Get out there and interact with the customer.

In many cases, the end user is not the person who makes the purchase decision. As we noted, college students are Lazybones users, but their parents make the purchase decision and write the check. Each of these players has a different motivation, and you, as the entrepreneur, need to be aware of each motivation so that you can design a product or service that meets each player's needs. For example, students want clean clothes without damage or loss, while parents want to insure that their kids are wearing clean underwear. In the case of Lazybones, the universities can act as influencers. If Lazybones secures a university endorsement, the university will include company information in the initiation materials it sends students before they enroll. This endorsement acts as a positive influencer that will garner trust from the parents. Understanding how all of these users, influencers, and actual buyers interact with each other will help you design the product or service that best meets their needs.

---

[19]In the age of fraud, as evidenced by Bernie Madoff, CountryWide Mortgage, etc., we can't stress enough the need to act in an ethical manner. When talking to competitors, never misrepresent yourself as a customer. Many of your competitors started out as entrepreneurs as well, and they understand the difficulties you are facing, so often they will freely talk to you except in the most competitive, cutthroat industries.

Lazybones Customer Section

SECTION 2: THE OPPORTUNITY

2.1 Customers

Highlights the user demographics. Matches the traditional university student at more affluent colleges. This will impact market size for the Lazybones offering. Dan needs to be prepared to address this in a presentation.

Our customers are 17- to 22-year-olds, typically from high-income families,

Highlights user psychographics. Students wear brand names, and their clothes are very important to them, which is further discussed in the following pages.

Note that the section also highlights the other piece of the customer puzzle. The payer.

Notice that Lazybones acknowledges a hurdle in the selling proposition. Within the marketing plan, they need to talk more about how they overcome this reluctance to try the service.

willing to pay a premium for service. Their clothes tend to be brand name from department stores and are very important to them. Parents pay for their children's services and often handle all of the arrangements throughout the semester. It is fairly common for a student wanting a laundry pickup to contact his mother who then will contact us and request that pickup. We act as an intermediate step between a heavily parented home life and an independent adult life.

Lazybones customers tend to have a considerable amount of money invested in their clothes but also considerable "sunk costs" in their wardrobes in the form of time, research, and the opinions of friends and family. The Lazybones customer does not see a pair of jeans as simply a replaceable item. Many of our customers regard the outsourcing of their laundry to be a risk that outweighs the inconvenience of having to do it themselves or taking it home.

Lazybones has also identified its primary influencer.

As a result, we have historically needed to rely on word-of-mouth for sales growth until a location reaches a certain critical mass. Another source that can provide our customers with confidence in our service is a university endorsement.

If a university trusts and recommends our service to interested students, it conveys quality and diminishes the perceived risk that our service might lose or damage their clothes. Universities compete for students and having a laundry service like Lazybones can be a feature that tilts a student's decision toward attending that university.

> This also shows why universities might be motivated to endorse Lazybones.

Competition

The competitive analysis is derived directly from the customer analysis. Specifically, you have previously identified your market segment and described what the customer looks like and what the customer wants. The key factor leading to the competitive analysis is what the customer wants in a particular product. These product attributes form a basis of comparison against your direct and indirect competitors. A competitive profile matrix is a useful tool to communicate those attributes and how the competition is currently addressing them. The matrix figure not only creates a powerful visual catch-point, it conveys information regarding gaps in the current offerings, setting the stage to describe your competitive advantage and the basis for your company's strategy. After a brief introductory paragraph, the competitive profile matrix should lead the section and be followed by text describing the analysis and its implications.

Creating a competitive profile matrix requires understanding of what the marketplace values; what is often called the key success factors. In other words, what makes the customer buy one company's product over another's? Think about a restaurant. People often choose to dine in restaurants based upon a number of factors, including location, price and quality of food, atmosphere, and so forth. Considering that you have a strong understanding of your customer, you should be able to identify what the key success factors are for your market space. Once you have the key success factors, you list your competition and your venture in the matrix and then evaluate how each company fairs in meeting the key success factors.

Finding information about your competition can be easy if the company is public, harder if it is private, and very difficult if the company is operating in "stealth" mode (it hasn't yet announced itself to the world). Most libraries have access to databases that contain a mother lode of information about publicly traded companies (see Fig. 4.2 for some sample sources), but privately held companies or those stealth ventures represent a greater challenge. The best way for savvy entrepreneurs to gather this information is through their network and via trade shows and to make purchases from the competitor. We know a large Burger King franchisee who eats at McDonald's once a month.

Who should be in the entrepreneur's network? First and foremost are the customers the entrepreneur hopes to sell to in the near future. Just as you are (or should be) talking to your potential customers, your existing competition is interacting with the customers every day, and your customers are likely aware of the stealth competition that is on the horizon. Although many entrepreneurs are fearful (verging on the brink of paranoia) that valuable information will fall into the wrong hands and lead to new competition that invalidates the current venture, the reality is that entrepreneurs who operate in a vacuum (meaning they don't talk to customers or show up at tradeshows, etc.) fail far more often than those who are talking to everybody they can. Talking allows entrepreneurs to get invaluable feedback that enables them to reshape their product offering before launching a product that may or may not be accepted by the marketplace. So network not only to find out about your competition but also to improve your own venture concept.

Once you have completed your competitor analysis, the stage is set to talk about your venture. For this reason, we suggest you include your venture in the matrix. It highlights where your venture expects to have a competitive advantage.

Figure 4.2 *Sample Source for Database Information on Public/Private Companies*

Infotrac — Index/Abstracts of journals, general business and finance magazines, market overviews, and profiles of public and private firms.

Capital IQ — Key people and contact info; company tear sheet; financial statements and ratios; suppliers/customers, M&A; stock prices.

Thomson ONE Banker — Company overview, history, analyst reports, deals, financial statements.

Business Source Complete — EBSCOhost — Find Datamonitor Company Reports, Company Profiles tab: SWOT analysis, competitors, summary.

ReferenceUSA — Search for companies by name or other criteria; create mailing lists; identify contacts. Many search criteria to find over 14 million company locations.

LexisNexis Academic — Business tab: overview, history, corporate structure, news, intellectual property.

Thomasnet.com — Directory of manufacturers, suppliers, and distributors. Search by industry, company name, brand, CAD drawings, and more. Includes links to Web sites and company catalogs.

Lazybones Competitor Section

2.2 Competition

Service Competitors

Lazybones competes with local laundromats that offer wash-and-fold laundry services and, in some new locations, laundry services that outsource the actual laundry (such as DormAid). Lazybones also competes with students doing their laundry themselves and with those students who live close enough to take their laundry home for Mom.

> Identifies the likely sources of competition. Note, also include those students who will do it themselves or take it home to Mom (assuming they live close enough).

> A secondary business, but not the key area where they compete.

> A competitive profile matrix gives a snapshot on how Lazybones stacks up. Note that this is from Dan's perspective and might be biased, but the following paragraphs explain his rationale. Be careful to include the key components of your business model and those of the competitors as a guide to the matrix components.

For storage, larger campuses typically have three or four providers in the area. These are generally local moving companies filling a need. A few national companies exist that aggregate student services, offer them over the Web, and then outsource the work out to local businesses.

Exhibit 2.1 *Competitive Profile Matrix*

	DIY (do it yourself)	Laundromats	Mom	DormAid	Lazybones
Quality	3	4	5	3	5
In House/ Outsource	In house	In Dorm	In house	Outsource	In house
Focus on College Student	2	5	5	5	5
Storage	1	3	3	1	5
Efficiency/Systems	3	2	3	4	5

Our business competes locally on five key factors, the combination of which is unique to Lazybones:

> One criticism of the five key success factors laid out here is that they are suited to what Lazybones does and don't include all the factors that would influence a customer's decision, such as price. Thus this analysis is biased. If Lazybones includes the key components of the competitor models they can rectify this problem.

1. <u>High quality control</u>: Anyone can do laundry. Washing, drying, folding, and delivering large quantities of laundry to a high level of quality is much more challenging than most people think, especially on a fixed budget. Many would-be competitors have gone out of business in a year or less, after learning this lesson the hard way. Lazybones has invested years of effort and nearly a quarter of a million dollars developing custom systems that allow us to efficiently process thousands of pounds of laundry each week to the high standards demanded by our customers.

2. <u>We do the work ourselves</u>: Some potential national competitors (like DormAid or the now defunct EZ Student Services) have beautiful marketing and Web presence, but they are farming out the actual laundry work (often to local students). As such they have little to no quality control to back it up. Unlike retail, the laundry business is dependent on ongoing weekly relationships. Marketing is key to bringing customers

> Appears to be another key success factor that Lazybones doesn't compare themselves against competitors on. Lazybones might note key quality assurance components in their system or even present customer satisfaction data from their 15 years of operations.

in, but long-term success depends on high retention rates and local recommendations to out-of-state parents.

3. <u>We focus on college students</u>: We remain laser-focused on a very specific, lucrative market. College students and their families are substantially wealthier than other

> This suggests that price may not be as important to these customers, although this is an assumption that needs testing.

Americans: U.S. college freshmen come from families with a median income 60 percent higher than the national average.[20]

Lazybones is focused on the wealthiest slice of this demographic at universities with the highest tuitions, aiming at students from families with incomes above $150,000/year.

4. We have strategic bundled services: We have integrated seasonal storage services for students into our business model. This leverages our relationships with out-of-state parents: caring for their child's laundry during the school year leads to our being trusted to care for their child's stuff during the summer. It then reinforces their desire to use us again for laundry in the fall. Storage also fills the summer-long seasonal gap, when the laundry slows dramatically; providing well-timed cash flow and allowing us to retain key personnel we would otherwise need to lay off.

5. There is a requirement for custom systems: Most businesses can buy off-the-shelf systems for tracking customer accounts. A dry cleaner, for instance, can choose from multiple systems. However, no such systems exist for the pickup-and-delivery laundry and storage market. Lazybones has invested years of effort and nearly a quarter of a million dollars developing custom systems, and any competitor will have to do the same to approach our level of organization, productivity tracking, and expense control.

> This key success factor is redundant with number 1 on quality control and could be a barrier to entry for competition.

A successful pickup-and-delivery business like Zoots could choose to duplicate our business model and compete head-to-head with us. The foregoing factors, however, illustrate that that is not a simple proposition. To compete effectively, they would need to invest a lot of time and money, and either focus as tightly as we do or risk being dramatically outperformed.

> In summary, the analysis is sound, but incomplete and biased. Generally, we prefer to do competitive analysis in a dispassionate, industry viewpoint. In this case, Dan has done it from the perspective of Lazybones.

[20]"American Freshman: 40 Year Trends 1966–2006" UCLA Newsroom, April 9, 2007. http://gseis.ucla.edu/heri/PDFs/PR_TRENDS_40YR.pdf.

Since Lazybones plans on growing via franchising, this competitive analysis is focused more on whether they can attract franchisees (customers), rather than whether the business model is attractive.

Franchise Competitors

Franchise-wise, Lazybones competes with a wide spectrum of companies. Any personal service company with relatively low start-up costs is an option our target franchisee could choose. These range from gift basket franchises like Edible Arrangements to trash removal franchises like 1-800-Junk-It.

Franchisees Advantages:

Identifies the key success factors that will drive a potential franchisee to franchise with Lazybones. Again, Dan could have used another competitive profile matrix to provide a snapshot of how Lazybones compares with other franchisors.

Our franchise opportunity stands out first and foremost as the only personal laundry service franchise available. Doing people's laundry is a simple chore that many franchise buyers feel they already understand and are qualified to perform. Compared to other franchises, personal laundry has the additional appeal of not requiring any handling of foods, hazardous chemicals, or dangerous equipment. Laundry and storage services have low barriers to entry and seem simple enough. Thus we must communicate a strong and well-defined value proposition to franchisees that clearly saves them more money than the fees they will pay us.

Our proven operations plan, strong brand, and multiple university endorsements mitigate an entrepreneur's risk and translate into faster and greater returns on upfront investments. Additionally, our knowledge and experience with laundry facilities translates into direct and quantifiable savings for franchisees:

- Getting the optimal mix of laundry machines can save a franchisee approximately $2,000 up front on installation and up to $100/month on utilities.

- Careful site selection and equipment installation will translate into savings of $2,000–$6,000.
- Inexpensive financing through our vendor can save a franchisee $8,000 on an equipment lease.
- Our professionally designed vinyl van wraps are available at a lower price and a higher quality than a franchisee could get on their own—saving a potential $2,000 per vehicle.
- Instant integration into our search engine–optimized Web site will provide real-time info to customers, handle orders, and process credit cards. Even a minimal Web site would cost a franchisee approximately $3,000. But ours also saves another 20 hours/week of administrative work, or $300/week at $15/hour.
- Our customer service personnel answer phones for franchisees. This saves at least 10 hours a week—or $150/week at $15/hour.
- Catering to a student market means extreme spikes in demand during move-in times for setting up laundry service and during move-out times for storage service. It is nearly impossible for a franchisee to staff up for these few weeks when call volumes more than quadruple. Missed calls translate into lost sales, and even three lost customers mean $500 in lost revenues per semester.

> Dan does a nice job of laying out the benefits to the franchisee. Using bullet points helps draw these favorable factors out. Dan might also have presented this as a table, tallying up the total value in savings that franchising with Lazybones would provide. Although this is effective, it really belongs in the section under Company, rather than Competition.

On a national franchise level our strongest advantages are in our financial numbers: 15–20 percent net profit margins and strong cash flows. Our systems and policies are designed around maximizing these strengths. We utilize simple and affordable technologies and a structured assembly line to maximize quality and minimize expenses. There are also very few franchises that cater to college campuses. These are points we feel would be relevant to franchisees with positive feelings about laundry, or a particular affinity toward a college campus. Another great advantage on the national franchise level is that Lazybones does not require a franchisee to have specific industry experience or a college education. Thanks to our sophisticated centralized systems and the simplicity of the basic business model, we can accommodate individuals with a high school education, a strong work ethic, and strong common sense. This is a tremendous advantage over businesses like restaurants and hotels where prior industry experience is a prerequisite for opening a franchise.

Chapter Summary

The industry, customer, and competition section of the plan lays the platform for you to introduce your vision. It is best to use a dispassionate tone. You need to present quantitative data (footnoting its source) to describe the industry, customer, and competitors. The more rigorously you describe and validate the context within which your venture will compete, the better you will understand how to compete. In other words, this portion of the business planning process is where you often gain your deepest learning. This deep learning will help you make better decisions. Furthermore, presenting this information well will strengthen your story and impress investors. Remember, when you build a house, everything rests upon the foundation. If that foundation is weak, the house will slowly crumble. This section of the plan is the foundation upon which the other sections build. Build it thoughtfully and completely.

5

COMPANY AND PRODUCT DESCRIPTION: SELLING YOUR VISION

Completing the dispassionate analysis described in Chapter 4 lays the foundation for describing your company and concept. This is the place to be passionate and sell your vision. Use both rational data and emotional appeals that support your story, but don't ramble. A concise, hard-hitting statement supported by data is impressive. Figure 5.1 lays out the major sections covered in this part of the plan. In the first paragraph identify the company name, where it is incorporated, and a brief overview of the concept for the company. Be clear but succinct in describing the product/service in this introductory paragraph. In the following paragraphs, you can go into much greater detail. The first paragraph should also highlight what the company has achieved to date; what milestones you have accomplished that show progress. Investors and stakeholders view much more favorably those action-oriented entrepreneurs who have accomplished milestones.

More space should be used to communicate the product. Again, graphic representations can be powerful. Reflecting on the competitive profile matrix from the previous section, highlight how your product fits into the customer value proposition. What is incorporated into your product and what added value do you deliver to the customer? This is sometimes called "the value proposition." This section should clearly

Figure 5.1 *Company and Product Description*

- Company description
- Product description
- Competitive advantage
- Entry strategy
- Growth strategy

and forcefully identify your venture's competitive advantage. Based upon your competitive analysis, why is your product better, cheaper, faster than what customers currently have access to? Your advantage may be a function of proprietary technology, patents, and distribution. In fact, the most powerful competitive advantages are derived from a bundle of factors because this makes them more difficult to copy. Lazybones claims that its competitive advantage is in its operations, refined over 15 years of operating experience. Like many businesses, success is a function of superior execution rather than some unique product attribute. While there are many competitors and substitutes to the Lazybones service, Dan has been successful because he can efficiently clean and return large quantities of laundry at a price that the customer is willing to pay. The lesson is that your competitive advantage may be hidden in how you provide the service, in addition to the service itself. On top of operational excellence, Lazybones's competitive advantage lies in understanding its customer. Students are newly departed from their home, and parents want to ease that transition. Thus Lazybones provides extensive customer service to ensure that the user (student) and payer (parent) are both happy with the product.

Once you have delineated your product, a perceptual map of your product and your competitors' products nicely communicates what makes your company special. Pick two or three of the key attributes identified in the competitor profile matrix and show how your venture differs from the competition. A competitor perceptual map visually illustrates what gaps in the market you expect to fill. We also suggest you bullet point the other elements that form the basis of your product/service competitive advantage.

As you can see, the business plan leads the reader in a logical progression. The goal is to create an understanding of your vision and make it tangible. So, again, we build from previous work, in this case our clear description of the product, to the strategy for introducing that product.

Many business plans falter here. They fail to articulate a clear entry strategy. Crafting a finely honed wedge to insert a new venture into a marketplace is essential for success. Think of taking a long walk. If you start on the wrong road the trip can be extended dramatically or you may never reach your destination. Therefore, the goal is to communicate how you enter the industry and survive for the first couple of years while you are building your customer base and refining your business model. Since most new ventures are resource constrained, especially in terms of available capital, it is crucial that the lead entrepreneur establish the most effective way to enter the market. Based upon analysis in the market and customer sections, entrepreneurs need to identify their primary target audience (PTA). Focusing on a particular subset of the overall market niche allows new ventures to effectively utilize scarce resources to reach those customers and prove the viability of their concept.

Lazybones may well be different from your business proposition in that Lazybones is attempting to grow an existing lifestyle business into a high-growth enterprise via franchising. Therefore, the plan talks about why people might want to become a franchisee, highlighting key points such as operating margins, refined systems, and a turnkey operation that will improve the franchisee's probability of success. However, this exercise is a clear example of explaining why the core idea is valuable for the broad set of stakeholders; operator, student, parent, university, among others.

The business plan should also sell the entrepreneur's vision for growth because that indicates the true potential for the business. Investors, in particular, need to assess the growth potential because that is what drives their returns. As part of the storytelling, you need to lay out the strategy and resultant scenario that you believe is most likely. Thus a paragraph or two should be devoted to the firm's growth strategy. If the venture achieves success in its entry strategy, it will either generate internal cash flow that can be used to fuel the growth strategy, or be attractive enough to get further equity financing at improved valuations. The growth strategy should talk about the secondary and tertiary target audiences that the firm will pursue. Thinking ahead to the next section of the business plan, the marketing section of the business plan must support your entry and growth strategies.

Lazybones Company Section

SECTION 3: COMPANY AND PRODUCT DESCRIPTION

3.1 Company Today

Company name, right up front.

Concise description of its milestones ... been in operations for over 15 years ... implying success in both operation and scaling of the opportunity.

Where it operates.

Lazybones has been in operation since 1993, when it first opened at the University of Wisconsin, Madison. Lazybones Syracuse opened in 1999, and Boston, Massachusetts, and Boulder, Colorado, locations opened in August 2008. Over the past 15 years Lazybones has refined, organized, expanded and streamlined its systems and its product mix in order to maximize its revenues and net margins and to accommodate absentee ownership.

Services

Concise description of the business concept. The next few paragraphs go into greater detail on its services.

Lazybones provides premium quality pickup and delivery laundry to college students, offering semester packages based on a pound limit. Upfront fees cover a student for one pickup each week of a semester up to a specified limit of laundry. Amounts over this limit are billed per pound. Pound limits are in 5-pound increments between 10 and 25 pounds per week. Lazybones does offer service in other ways: block of pounds packages (e.g., 100-, 200-, or 300-pound blocks) to be used at the purchaser's discretion with escalating discounts; and service by the pound without limits.

Laundry is picked up, separated into lights and darks, washed with top-quality liquid detergent and fabric softeners, dried, meticulously folded, packaged in brown paper, and delivered within 24 hours of pickup. Special requests for certain items, such as air drying or low-heat drying, or using hypoallergenic detergents or softeners, are handled at the customer's request.

Exhibit 3.1 *Lazybones Colorado Laundry Floor*

Lazybones offers dry cleaning too, charging by the item and subcontracting to a local dry cleaner.

Summer and semester abroad storage services are provided as well. Lazybones personnel come to the student's dorm room or apartment during a two-hour scheduled window. Any items to be stored are picked up and transported into storage for the summer. Items are packed and shipped as well upon request. Come fall, all items are returned during a prescheduled two-hour window.

Customer Service

Although Lazybones end users are college students, services are paid for predominantly by parents.

Out-of-state parents routinely set up and oversee their child's service arrangements and often hold us responsible for their child's unreliability. This creates unique customer service demands. In addition, the stressful start and end of the school years make for extreme—super seasonal—demands on the system; average call volumes of 30–40 calls per location during normal weeks skyrocket to over 500 per day during the busy seasons. Lazybones uses a centralized database to keep all information related to laundry and storage and uses a call center to provide its phone support. Additional hourly help is added during these peak times at the call center.

3.2 Franchise Product Proposition

Lazybones's 15–20 percent net profit margins are one of its many attractive qualities. Its carefully designed and developed systems mitigate risks associated with the extreme seasonality

> Notice how the plan provides a nuanced perspective of its customers. While students are the users, parents typically pay for the service. This understanding will drive the marketing strategy. Much of the effort will be geared toward the parent (which we will see in the next section of the plan).

> Since Lazybones is an existing business, this plan focuses on growth. While many of you reading this book will present a strategy to enter the market, the Lazybones strategy focuses on how to grow its presence in the market. In a new venture, your job is to compress the learning as best as possible through the use of networks, research, and customer understanding that we described earlier.

> In this paragraph, Lazybones lays out its value proposition for potential franchisees, namely high profit margins and proven operations.

of the business, optimize cash flows throughout the year, and narrow the demands on a franchisee to allow control of the bottom line.

The following sections summarize who our ideal franchise customers are, what franchisees will receive in return for their $125,000 upfront investment (which includes our $35,000 franchise fee), and explain how the fees have been chosen.

Franchise Customers

> This section lays out the psychographics of a typical Lazybones franchisee. Understanding your customer will help you devise a strategy to reach your potential customer. It would also be useful to identify likely demographics, such age, gender, net worth, and so on to gain a deeper picture of your customer.

Franchise buyers tend to be eager to run their own business and be their own boss, viewing this as a better source of job security than working for a large corporation. They want regular interaction with their customers, not an isolated desk job. They are looking for a reasonable income, rather than an opportunity to get filthy rich—though they certainly don't object to getting rich.

> Starts to suggest one demographic is experience (or lack thereof). The fact that the person doesn't need experience suggests that younger people, perhaps recent college grads, would be one prime demographic (this matches the experience that the founders had when they started their first Lazybones). In addition, this operation might be attractive to older career changers or people who have been displaced from their career.

The Lazybones franchisees we want share these characteristics, plus a few more. They are looking for a hands-on role, and are eager to get their hands dirty. In other words, they want to run the franchise themselves, not hire a manager to do it for them. They are looking for a business where they can deliver a tangible product. Perhaps what is most unique about Lazybones, though, is what we do *not* require of our franchisees. Many franchises, like restaurants, require that their franchisees have significant prior experience in that industry. This is not true for Lazybones; we have no need for franchisees to have experience with laundry or storage. In fact, we have no specific minimum education or experience requirements.

> Some investors will see this as a double-edged sword—inexperience will increase training cost and could affect quality. The entrepreneurs need to understand both edges of the business model component and be prepared to answer questions. Subway is an example of a franchise that doesn't require experience and has had phenomenal success.

Anyone who has demonstrated the ability to be a self-starter, has a great work ethic, and can raise the relatively modest investment required to start a Lazybones is a worthy candidate. We are confident that the great flexibility we demonstrate in our franchisee requirements will allow us to find great candidates more quickly and easily than our franchise competitors.

Exhibit 3.2   *Venn Diagram of Ideal Lazybones Franchise Buyers*

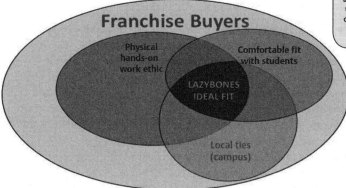

Diagrams are an excellent way to summarize the prose and add depth to a plan. From this graphic, we get a glimpse of another ideal demographic, geographic proximity to the campus of operation.

Our franchises will be positioned on the lower end of the initial investment spectrum (Exhibit 3.3), and we will offer financing to help us target franchisees looking for a business that will require more hard work than capital.

A sophisticated investor will flag this statement and look at both capital requirement impact and increased risk in the deal.

This perceptual map gives a sense of how Lazybones will compete for franchisees. It is looking for individuals who have lower income and are seeking a lower initial investment. Buying and establishing a McDonald's franchise, for instance, typically runs over $2 million. McDonald's requires franchisees to have $250,000 cash for an individual restaurant. Real estate investment and equipment leases can add another $2 million, often financed. Lazybones might be advised to add more service franchises to the comparables. Service Master would be a good example.

Exhibit 3.3   *Lazybones Franchise Positioning Map*

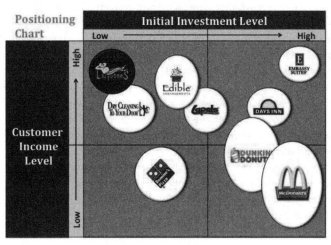

The following sections provide greater detail on what Lazybones is "selling" to the franchisees. Be careful to prioritize this message based on customer perception of importance.

Turnkey On-Site Operational Systems Including the Following:

- High-efficiency "green" commercial laundry equipment optimally sized and selected for services
- Custom site design maps and layout of equipment, staff, and workflow
- Licensed and professional installation by plumbers and electricians
- Computers, routers, card swipers, and barcode scanners for laundry and storage workstations
- Detailed operational instructions for each workstation in the laundry and storage processes
- Handheld scanning units for work done in the field
- Video surveillance systems with Web integration for offsite monitoring and reviewing
- Global Positioning System and associated software for tracking the location of franchisee's delivery vans

Investors will look for how these central functions scale and create economies of scale.

Access to Centralized Functions:

- A Web database system for managing the entire operation, automatically tracking invoices, customers, processes, and employee work hours, as well as processing credit card sales transactions into franchisee bank accounts. This database includes tools for identifying problems with a customer's laundry (lost items for instance), for communicating those problems to key members of the organization, and for tracking them to solution. The database is also set up to post sales invoices and payment data directly to QuickBooks accounting software.
- A central Web site and server for answering customer questions and registering new customers and taking their payments.
- Integration with our customer service phone bank for taking customer orders and receiving and handling customer complaints and concerns. Use of the call center is an additional fee for franchisees and is intended as extra support during extreme seasonal times, during times when the service is short staffed, or when customer traffic simply reaches higher-than-normal volumes.
- An online communications hub for use by both franchisees and company store managers. This will include a complete directory of email addresses, cell phone numbers, and online chat addresses; a suggestion blog maintained by the company's franchising personnel; and a discussion bulletin board. The chat features of the company are integrated at each workstation to facilitate rapid response time in a fast-paced environment.
- As the local franchise grows, our system provides efficiency reports and extensive metrics with which franchise owners can better evaluate, manage, and motivate their staffs. Payroll efficiency in this labor-intensive industry is directly linked with any franchisee's bottom line.

Exhibit 3.4 *Screenshot of Laundry Weigh Station*

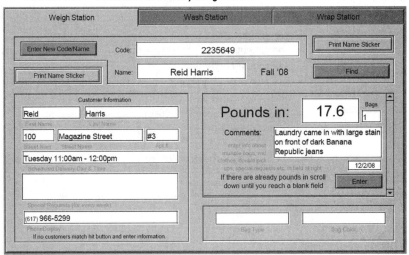

Training and Start-Up Support:

- All franchisees will travel to Boston for a two-week training session. The session will include observing and participating in all the critical operations of the Boston company store and Lazybones headquarters.
- An experienced Lazybones employee will spend two weeks on site assisting each franchisee before the official opening day.
- Administrative and accounting support for common items including sales and use tax filings, Department of Transportation issues, and child support for employees.

Marketing Strategy and Materials:

- Marketing strategy, budget constraints, and overview materials based on 15 years of marketing
- Professionally designed location signs
- Extensive graphics (vinyl wraps) for company vehicles
- Brochures, flyers, posters, T-shirts, etc., for initial marketing on campus
- Mailing labels for direct mail to parents
- Contact packets and other materials for establishing university relationships
- Professionally designed and maintained Web site optimized for searches relating to franchisee's services and campus
- Web marketing on Facebook and Google both for the brand and for the franchisee's campus
- Digital library of different flyers, print ads, brochures, etc.

> Before leaving the previous section on product attributes, a perceptual map showing how the Lazybones franchisee stacks up on two key attributes, such as profit margins and operational support, would help communicate why this is especially attractive to potential franchisees. Visuals add to your overall plan readability.

3.3 Site Evaluators

We believe a few key elements combine to make a suitable Lazybones location:

- Enrollment above 2,500 students (each student represents a potential customer)
- Greater than 20 percent out-of-state students (historically better customers)
- Tuition rates above $18,000, resulting in high-income student families

A city in which multiple schools with these traits are close to one another may be an even more attractive location.

Chapter Summary

The industry, customer, competition section sets the platform. The company and product section is the place to passionately sell your story. Communicate why you believe that you have a compelling product. Tell us about its competitive advantage. Present a persuasive entry strategy followed by an exciting growth strategy. Whereas the foundation of most houses is cement and buried under ground, the house itself should show your style. Let your passion for the vision come through.

6 MARKETING PLAN: REACHING THE CUSTOMER

We have set the stage for your company's potential to success-fully enter and grow in a marketplace. Now we need to devise the strategy that will allow the company to reach its potential. Figure 6.1 highlights the major sections of the marketing plan. Let's look at each of these subsections in turn.

Target Market

Every marketing plan needs some guiding principals. Based upon the knowledge gleaned from the target market analysis, entrepreneurs need to position their product accordingly. All product strategies reflect a belief that customer purchases are on a continuum stretching from rational pur-chases to emotional purchases. As an example, when one buys a new car, the rational purchase might be a low-cost, reliable car such as the Ford Fiesta. However, there is an emotional element as well. You want the car

Figure 6.1 *Marketing Plan*
- The target market strategy
- The product/service strategy
- Pricing strategy
- Distribution strategy
- Advertising and promotion
- Sales strategy
- Sales and marketing forecasts.

to be an extension of your personality. So, based upon your economic means and self-perception, you buy a 1965 Ford Mustang Convertible because of the emotional benefits you derive. Within every product space, there is room for products at different points along the continuum. Entrepreneurs need to decide where their product fits (or where they would like to position it) as this influences the other aspects of the marketing plan.

Lazybones, for instance, tends toward the emotional side of the continuum. Parents could insist that their children do their own laundry. It would be more economical, but parents want to ease their child's transition to college and insure that their child dresses presentably. Thus Lazybones is counting on parents making an emotional decision; therefore, their marketing plan will tug on those sentiments.

Figure 6.2

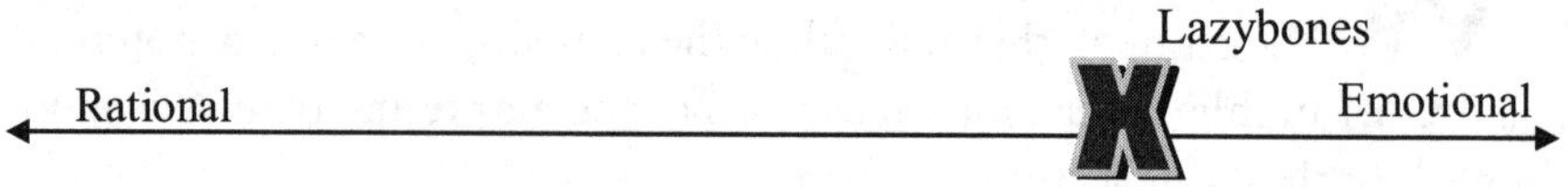

Rational ←——————————————— 𝕏 ——→ Emotional

Lazybones

Product/Service Strategy

Building from the target market definition, this section of the plan describes how your product is differentiated from that of the competition. It's informative to look back on the competitive dimensions you described in the competitive profile matrix. What attributes are important to the customers? Are they willing to pay a premium for those features? Will they continue to pay a premium for those features? One of the biggest mistakes entrepreneurs make is evaluating an opportunity as if it were static. But marketplaces change; customer values change. Think about cell phones; in the early years people paid huge premiums for the hardware and the minutes. As the product became more widely dispersed, price became an ever increasingly important attribute. Wireless companies began giving away the hardware and enticing customers with great calling plans. They try to make up for the lost revenue through data plans, but as smartphones proliferate, expect those rates to decrease too. The point is that if you had entered the market early and viewed it in a static fashion, falling prices would have caught you by surprise and potentially led to your firm's demise. So, as you think about your product/

service strategy, try to identify those attributes that have the potential to be sustainable. What will the customer value over the long run?

You will need to consider other issues as well. Discuss why the customer will switch to your product and how you will retain customers so that they don't switch to your competition in the future. This section should also address how you will provide service to the customer. What type of technical support will you provide? Will you offer warranties? What kind of product upgrades will be available and when? It is important to detail all these efforts, as they must all be accounted for in the pricing of the product. Many times, entrepreneurs underestimate the costs of these services, which leads to a drain on cash flow and can ultimately lead to bankruptcy.

Pricing Strategy

Determining how to price your product is always difficult. The two primary approaches are the "cost plus" approach and the "market demand" approach. We advise entrepreneurs to avoid cost plus pricing. It is difficult to accurately determine your actual cost, especially if this is a new venture with a limited history. New ventures consistently underestimate the true cost of developing their products. For example, how much did it really cost to write that software? The cost would include salaries and payroll tax burden, computer and other assets, overhead contribution, and so forth. Since most entrepreneurs underestimate these costs,[1] there is a tendency to underprice the product. Another pricing strategy that gets entrepreneurs in trouble is to offer a low price so that they can penetrate and gain market share rapidly. There are problems with a low price: it may be difficult to raise the price later, demand at that price may overwhelm your ability to produce the product in sufficient volume, and it may unnecessarily strain cash flow. Also, low price may connote lower value versus the competition. Therefore, the better method is to canvass the market and determine an appropriate price based upon what the competition is currently offering and how your product is positioned. If you are offering a low-cost-value product, price below market rates. If your product is of better quality or has features superior to those of the competition (the more common case), it should be priced at a premium to the competition.

---

[1]The fluid nature of the start-up firm means that purchasing power, changing product or service components, and even the offering itself make the real and total cost of a product very difficult to pin down.

Distribution Strategy

This section identifies how you will reach the customer. Many new ventures assume the availability and capacity of channels of distribution for a new "improved" product. That's almost always a mistake. One of the authors had a friend who developed chili in a jar. The entrepreneur had extensive experience in packaged foods, previously having worked for a large national food conglomerate and more recently with a successful beverage start-up. Although the product was of high quality (as good as making it from scratch and much better than chili in a can), the entrepreneur found it impossible to break into the grocery store distribution channel in a significant way. The large food processors control all the shelf space. So even though the product was new and improved, it did not survive.

It is also important to understand the cost of reaching the customer, even if you can access the distribution channels. The e-commerce boom of the late 1990s assumed that the growth in Internet usage and purchases would create new demand for pure Internet companies. Yet the distribution strategy for many of these firms did not make sense. Pets.com and other online pet supply firms had a strategy where the pet owner would log on, order the product from the site, and then receive delivery via UPS or the U.S. Postal Service. In theory this works, except that the price the market would bear for this product didn't cover the exorbitant shipping costs of a 40-pound bag of dog food.

It is wise to examine how the customer currently acquires the product. If your customer buys dog food at Petco, then you might use independent retail outlets to sell a new brand of dog food and migrate to a big box player as you gain brand recognition. This is not to say that entrepreneurs might not develop a multichannel distribution strategy, but if they want to achieve maximum growth, at some point they will have to use common distribution techniques or reeducate the customer about where and how to buy their product (which can be very expensive). If you determine that Petco is the best distribution channel, the next question is, can you access it? As a new start-up in dog food, it may be difficult to get shelf space at Petco. That may suggest an entry strategy of boutique pet stores to build brand recognition. The key here is to identify appropriate channels and then assess how costly it is to access them.

Lazybones has two distribution strategies. First, it can reach out to students directly. Its advertising strategy would support this distribution by placing flyers around campus, putting ads in university publications, and so on.

However, since the primary target is the parent, Lazybones has found that a better strategy is to be endorsed by the university, which then promotes and includes Lazybones advertisements in the information packets it sends to parents. In essence, Lazybones is distributing its service through the university.

Advertising and Promotion

Communicating effectively to your customer requires advertising and promotion. Referring again to the dot-com boom of the late nineties, the defunct Computer.com made a classic mistake in its attempt to build brand recognition. It blew over half of the venture capital it raised on a series of expensive Super Bowl ads for the January 2000 event ($3 million of $5.8 million raised on three Super Bowl ads).[2] Resource-constrained entrepreneurs need to carefully select the appropriate strategies. What avenues most effectively reach your primary target audience (PTA)? If you can identify your PTA by names, then direct sales approaches, such as direct mail or e-mail, may be more effective. Try to utilize grassroots techniques such as public relations efforts geared toward mainstream media. Sheri Poe, founder of Ryka women's shoes, appeared on the Oprah Winfrey show, touting shoes for women, designed by women. The response was overwhelming. In fact, she was so besieged by demand, she couldn't supply enough shoes.

It is important to distinguish between early-stage advertising strategies and those that will emerge as your company grows. For example, one of the authors was on the founding team for Jiffy Lube. In the early days, the company used direct mail (coupons) to all registered vehicle owners. As the company grew nationally, it switched to radio advertisements because people listened to the radio when they were driving, and they were more likely to think about the need for an oil change. The key is to develop an appropriate strategy based upon your PTA and the stage of your company's development.

As you develop a multipronged advertising and promotion strategy, create detailed schedules that show which avenues you will pursue and the associated costs. These types of schedules serve many purposes, including providing accurate cost estimates, which will help in assessing how much capital you need to raise. These schedules also build credibility

---

[2]O. Sacribey, "Private Companies Temper IPO Talk," *IPO Reporter*, December 18, 2000. Page 9.

in the eyes of potential investors because they show that you understand the nuances of your industry.

Sales Strategy

This section provides the backbone that supports all of the above. Specifically, it illustrates what kind and level of human capital you will devote to the effort. How many salespeople and how much customer support do you need? Will these people be internal to the organization or outsourced? If they are internal, will there be a designated sales force or will different members of the company serve in a sales capacity at different times? Again, this section builds credibility if the entrepreneur demonstrates an understanding of how the business should operate. In our pet food example a start-up could use a direct sales force or a series of pet food distributors. Of course, a blend of the two sales strategies is also possible.

Sales Forecasts

Gauging the impact of the foregoing efforts is difficult. Nonetheless, to build a compelling story, entrepreneurs need to show projections of revenues well into the future. How do you derive these numbers? There are two methods, the comparable method and the buildup method. The comparable method models sales forecasts after what other companies have achieved, adjusting for age of company, variances in product attributes, support services such as advertising and promotion, and so forth. After detailed investigation of the industry and market, entrepreneurs know the competitive players and have a good understanding of their history. In essence, the entrepreneur monitors a number of comparable competitors and then explains why her business varies from those models.

Lazybones has an advantage over a brand new startup. Specifically, they have an operating history at their existing laundries. In essence, Dan will take the performance of one of his typical stores and use that as a comparable for all new franchisees Lazybones secures. The buildup method, in this case, is the number of franchisees that Lazybones expects to sell each year. So one might argue that Lazybones doesn't need to benchmark with comparable companies, but that would be a mistake. Moving from four company operations to a franchisee network will require new infrastructure. Their knowledge of the "unit economics" allows them to understand how fast and to what size a franchised operation should grow at any given location. Also, instead of having a corporate operation of three people (Dan, his cofounder Reg, and newly hired Joel), Lazybones will need to build a corporate infrastructure to support its franchisees. The strategy will be to create marketing economies on a regional and national level. Benchmarking other franchise operations and identifying how quickly they scaled from a few company-owned operations to a nationwide network will help Dan develop realistic projections.

In the buildup method, the entrepreneur identifies all the revenue sources and then estimates how much of each revenue type the start-up can generate per day, or some other small time period. The buildup technique is an imprecise method for the new startup with limited operating history, but it is critically important to assess the viability of the opportunity. So important in fact, that we advise entrepreneurs to use both the comparable and buildup techniques to assess how well they converge. If the two methods are widely divergent, go back through and try to determine why. The deep knowledge you gain of your business model will greatly help you articulate the opportunity to stakeholders, as well as manage the business when it is launched.

There is a plethora of information about franchising companies that Lazybones can use to implement a buildup revenue and unit growth projection. The Federal Trade Commission requires franchisors to complete a Franchise Disclosure Document (FDD).[3] Item 19 of the FDD calls for a disclosure of franchise revenues. Additionally, a number of states require more detailed disclosure. Lazybones could look at a number of franchise operations that have taken different growth paths. The popular press also provides interesting data for a potential franchise company. In particular Lazybones might look at *Entrepreneur Magazine*'s Franchise 500[4] issue. They have been ranking franchises by quantitative data for about 30 years. Also, *Franchise Times* compiles its own annual Top 200 Franchise Chains list, which is based on worldwide sales.

Because Lazybones has 15 years of experience they would start with the data from their current operations. The company has to decide whether they are going to grow regionally (like Dunkin Donuts when they started) or nationally (Subway). Then they would project how economies of

---

[3] www.ftc.gov/opa/1995/10/unfr.shtm.
[4] www.entrepreneur.com/franchise500/index.html.

scale in marketing would increase the ramping up of historical revenue patterns.

We can use the buildup method to validate the Lazybones projections. Historically, they achieve location sales of approximately $200,000 in year one and $370,000 in year two. While there is widely different scale impact, our experience has been that a franchise will break even in 18 months and achieve 15–20 percent faster revenue increases than a stand-alone operation. College Hunks Hauling Junk[5] is an interesting comparable. It is a relatively young, service franchise that has grown to 30 franchise locations and growing within its first five years. The company employs college students and recent grads in its junk hauling/recycling operations. It appears that College Hunks does about $40,000 in sales per employee. We then compared this to Lazybones projections for a typical store and find that Lazybones is projecting revenue of $56,000 per employee in year five. Thus the Lazybones projections seem reasonable.

	Sales per Store	Employees	Sales/Employee
Lazybones Yr 1	$200,000	5	$40,000
Lazybones Yr 2	$370,000	7	$52,857
Lazybones Yr 5	$730,000	13	$38,666
College Hunks[6]	$2.9	75	$38,666

The one thing we know for certain is that these forecasts will never be 100 percent accurate, but the question is the degree of error. Detailed investigation of comparable companies reduces that error. Triangulating the comparable results with the buildup results reduces that error further. The smaller the error, the less likely the company will run out of cash. Also, rigorous estimates build an intimate understanding of the forces that will affect revenue and credibility with your investors. We should point out that, although Lazybones projections seem optimistic, this is pretty common. Entrepreneurs always believe things will happen more quickly and with less cost than is typically the case. We would expect that in future iterations of the plan, Lazybones will develop stronger projections based upon investor, franchisee, and operating experience feedback. Nonetheless, going through the preceding exercises gives you the ammunition to convince investors and others that your projections are reasonable.

---

[5]www.1800junkusa11.reachlocal.com/.
[6]College Hunks sales are overall sales, not per store. Considering that College Hunks is still young and doesn't have many units, we expect that most of the employees are providing the service, rather than corporate overhead. Data pulled from InfoTrac Company Profiles.

Lazybones Marketing Plan

SECTION 4: MARKETING PLAN

Lazybones is in the business of selling premium services to college students, and Lazybones is in the business of selling its business model to qualified franchisees. Effectively doing the second depends largely on the effectiveness of doing the first.

Our experience with college students has shown that sales success is much more dependent on quality and convenience than on marketing spend. Word of mouth and the endorsements of the universities where we operate are historically the main drivers. As such, reaching a critical mass nationally will increase our ability both to secure these endorsements and to reach out to incoming freshmen around the country. Our goal is to reach target customer levels on each campus as quickly as possible and to expand to a maximum number of campuses via franchising without compromising our brand's reputation for quality. We intend to achieve this by centralizing the parts of the business that require more in-depth education and seeking out and training managers and franchisees who will be focused on hands-on delivery of our services to end users.

4.1 On Campus

Pricing Strategy

The price of the laundry service is seldom the key decision point for our customers.

If the quality and reliability of the service are there, they are happy to pay a premium. There is an additional social factor attached to our service: students typically want to do what their friends are doing. These factors work heavily in our favor in the long term, but against us in the short term. Due to the relative price inelasticity, customers cannot be attracted simply by discounting.

> This is a statement of the product/service strategy. Interesting that they do not say premium *laundry* service, but premium services. This implies that Dan has a view toward increasing their share of college students' disposable income, by adding storage services, for instance. This statement leaves open the option that they will add further services in the future.

> There are over 7,000 higher education institutions in the United States, with over 15 million students, according to U.S. Department of Education statistics. This might be a good place to reinforce the size of this opportunity.

> This section identifies at a high level corporate versus franchise strategy. Corporate will centralize aspects, such as operational design and creating a unifying brand, and franchisees will focus on service delivery.

> Notes that their target customer is price insensitive. Also points out that students like to mimic their friends. This has important implications for the rest of the marketing strategy.

> Telling the reader some negatives, especially when you have an answer to the problem, illustrates a detailed understanding of the market.

> Based upon the premium price strategy, Lazybones identifies some marketing strategies that might entice students to try the service. Notice how they are using social institutions to get at a student's desire to do what their friends are doing.

When opening on a campus we must be aggressive in acquiring customers and dedicate ourselves to their satisfaction so that they will consistently endorse us to their friends. Our pricing will be at a premium level, but we need to be very creative and aggressive about discounting during the first year of operations. Offering group specials aimed at getting fraternities and sororities to try us out, and offering giveaways as part of promotional advertising are effective techniques. We also need to be extremely flexible and accommodating to customer requests in order to remove their reluctance to try our service.

Our service will be largely sold in the form of semester packages with pound limits attached (10, 15, 20, or 25 pounds per week). This is also beneficial to our cash flow. We will sell blocks of pounds at discounted rates and also offer straight laundry by the pound (Exhibit 4.1).

Storage is priced by the piece—flat fees for typical items like boxes and plastic bins—and charges per cubic inch for items that vary in size like furniture. All prices are for the pickup and the storage of the items, although we do add a delivery fee of $25 for customers who do not schedule their delivery by midsummer. Typical charges are around $40 for a box, and the customer average for an order is around $250. We do not sell "packages" to students with certain numbers of boxes included but rather take whatever items they end up with for storage.

> This exhibit nicely summarizes Lazybones pricing. If Lazybones added a column with the expected percentage of customers choosing each package, it would help them refine their revenue projections. This is great comparable data to share with franchisees.

Exhibit 4.1   *Laundry Pricing*

Package	Price	Extra Pounds
Semester Laundry Packages		
10 lb per week	$229.00	$1.59
15 lb per week	$299.00	$1.59
20 lb per week	$369.00	$1.59
25 lb per week	$429.00	$1.59
Block of 100 lb	$109.00	$1.59
Block of 200 lb	$198.00	$1.59
Block of 300 lb	$367.00	$1.59
Laundry by the pound		$1.79

Reaching the Customer

There are two primary ways of reaching the customer. The first is to directly approach students on campus by reaching out to fraternities and sororities as mentioned earlier. However, since parents ultimately make the buying decision, reaching them through university endorsement is often more effective. We need to earn university endorsements, so we first need a critical mass of students. It is the role of the franchisee to go and sell the service on the campus. Lazybones will provide the franchisees sales training as well as brochures, flyers, and advertising via Google and Facebook to support their efforts.

In exchange for a university endorsement, the mailing labels for freshman and sophomore students, a link on the school Web site, and the use of the front desks in dormitories, we will pay a commission to University Housing on each student we service. We use this strategy at Syracuse and a similar agreement with the landlords of the privately owned dorms on the University of Wisconsin's campus. These agreements solidify an effective monopoly on campus. Universities are typically more concerned with our reliability and quality of service than with the money we will generate for them, and this is why it took about two years to earn the endorsement in Syracuse. We expect that once the company reaches a certain critical size and level of brand recognition, these endorsements will come more quickly.

As a service business, distribution is often direct. In this section, Lazybones lays out its distribution strategy, focusing on on-campus efforts as well as securing university endorsement. A product business, on the other hand, would rely on different distribution channels, such as retailers.

A table showing what these costs typically are by item (brochure, flyer, etc.) over the first several years of a franchise's life would help Lazybones strengthen its pro forma projections. We suggest putting such a table in the marketing plan. It will directly correlate to the marketing expenses in the financials.

Notice how their distribution strategy strives for a competitive advantage. Lock up the university channel through commissions and it becomes more difficult for competitors to supplant Lazybones. Sophisticated investors will ask about contract length so Lazybones should be ready with an answer.

Exhibit 4.2: *Full-Body Vehicle Graphics*

Pictures throughout the plan are good visual catch-points that draw the reader in.

Their communications strategy is discussed in very broad terms. It is often useful to include a schedule detailing the various types of communications, where those communications will appear, and how much it will cost to place them. This advertising expense table then feeds directly into the pro forma financials.

Communications Strategy

Our company cargo van is one of our best sources of advertising. We invest in full-body, brightly colored graphics for our vehicles to maximize their visibility as they make loops around campus 40 hours or more each week (Exhibit 4.2). This consistent, tangible presence around campus is critical to getting the word out and helping to bolster the "everyone else is doing it" mentality.

College students are a particularly easy target for promotions because they have consistent move-in days and predictable annual schedules.

We also use promotions, offering laundry packages for giveaways as prizes at local events, and incentivizing our own customers via credits and discounts to recruit friends to try the service.

Again, a table showing these expected expenses would lead to stronger financial projections and provide a visual catch-point.

Our centralized Web site will be tuned (via search engine optimization) to appear on the first page of laundry-related searches at each campus, and we will invest in Web marketing through Google Adwords and Facebook. We will also pursue customers via Twitter marketing and be aggressive in using all new communications technologies as they arise.

Since Lazybones has two different customers, it has a separate section discussing franchisees.

4.2 Franchise Sales

Benchmarking the franchise fee in a table would add credibility to their claim and also communicate how the fee might change over time. For instance, as Lazybones becomes a stronger brand in the marketplace, we would expect it to raise its franchise fee in accordance with other strongly branded franchisors.

Franchise Pricing

In return for all these benefits, franchisees will need to make an upfront investment of approximately $125,000. This is toward the low end of required franchise investments across the industry. We will connect franchisees with potential sources to get the majority of this financed. Part of the initial investment is a franchise fee of $35,000. This is slightly above the industry average of $25,000, but what will matter most for a franchisee is the total initial set-up cost, which is lower than the industry average. Our research indicates we are offering substantially more benefits to franchisees than our competitors who charge lower fees.

This suggests that Lazybones may be underpricing its franchise. Typically, the more benefits you offer, the higher your price. A table of benchmark franchisors would help place this in context and make it easier to validate Lazybones pricing.

Furthermore, unlike many competitors, we do not require our franchisees to purchase any specific equipment or supplies from us.

This is a double-edged sword. Required product purchase usually results from national purchasing accounts that embed competitive advantage because you are providing your franchisees needed supplies at a lower price than they could secure on their own.

Franchises will also need to contribute 7 percent of their monthly revenue to Lazybones corporate. This contribution is slightly above the industry average of 5.5 percent, but, again, we believe we are offering more benefits to compensate. Specifically, we are confident franchisees can make larger net margins with Lazybones than with most other franchises. For instance, dry cleaners and Laundromats average net margins between 3 and 6 percent, while Lazybones has historically achieved 15–20 percent.

> A table showing how Lazybones stacks up on these metrics versus competition would be very compelling. It should also be in materials they present to these customers.

Asking for a 1.5 percent larger contribution in exchange for a three- to fivefold improvement in net margins is a very fair exchange.

Exhibit 4.3: *Franchising Pricing Table*

> Franchise fee = higher than average
> Royalty = higher than average
> Ad fee = lower than average

Franchise fee	$35,000
Royalty rate	7% of revenues
Advertising rate	1% of revenues

Franchisees will also need to contribute 1 percent of their monthly revenue into a national advertising fund. This goes into a fund that is jointly managed by headquarters and a council of franchisees, and used for nationwide advertising. This is a standard approach in the franchising industry.

Communications

We have had numerous franchise requests over the last 10 years, despite neither advertising this opportunity nor being ready to provide it. Nearly all of these requests came from parent customers. Therefore, the first place we will look for potential franchisees is from this pool of people already familiar with us.

> Integrating the franchising advertising into material the firm already produces is a cost-effective means of getting your message out. It is basically free.

We will integrate the franchise message with our current marketing materials nationwide, adding summary information about franchising opportunities to the mailers we send out to parents each year. We will also place mentions of our franchising business on every package of laundry we deliver, the packaging for everything we ship or store, and the invoices sent to our customers.

> There is a cost to SEO. A table summarizing all these efforts and their associated costs powerfully communicates the Lazybones strategy and leads to more accurate financial projections.

Besides aggressively marketing franchises to the parents and students who are our customers, we will also implement a thorough online marketing campaign. A link from our main Web page will connect to an extensive Web site devoted to franchising. We will do extensive search engine optimization (SEO) so that this Web site appears high up in Google searches for low-cost franchising and laundry franchising. We will also advertise with Google Adwords and on the most popular franchising Web sites such as franchise.org and franchising.com. Our personnel will become active participants in the International Franchising Association and on online franchise social networking sites. Finally, we will make aggressive efforts to work the press at all levels. We will solicit stories in college and local newspapers and issue regular press releases whenever new locations open.

We will make it as easy as possible for franchisees to get information on Lazybones. They can download detailed information, including our Franchise Disclosure Documents (FDDs), from the Web site in return for providing their contact information. Alternately, they can dial a toll-free number to request this information. Our personnel will also be available via the phone or via live Web chat to answer potential franchisee questions.

Chapter Summary

Many people consider the marketing plan to be the most important part of the planning process because it communicates how you will reach the customer. As we discuss later in the book, successfully reaching your customer is often the most critical risk a new venture faces. As such, investors will look at this part of the plan to see if you have a credible strategy. That means looking at the distribution channels, pricing, and advertising plans. The more detail you provide, the more credibility you build. As such, liberally use tables to highlight advertising outlets and costs, sales and marketing head counts, and salaries. Spend the time to get these details right because it means that you will have a stronger grasp on your major operating expenses and your road to profitability.

7 OPERATIONS AND DEVELOPMENT: EXECUTION

Operations Plan

The operations section of the plan has progressively shortened as more companies outsource nonvital aspects of their production. For a service company like Lazybones, on the other hand, the operations plan tends to be more detailed as it shows how the company provides its service to the customer. Figure 7.1 illustrates the main sections of the operations plan. The key in this section is to articulate operational competitive advantages and address how operations will add value to your customers. Furthermore, the section details the production cycle, allowing the entrepreneur to gauge the cycle's impact on working capital. The "cash conversion cycle" is always a point of concern for a start-up.[1] For instance, when does the company pay for inputs? How long does it take to produce the product? When does the customer buy the product and, more importantly, when does the customer pay for the product? The time from the beginning of this process until the product is paid for will drain cash flow and has implications for financing.

---

[1]CCC = number of days between distributing cash and collecting cash in connection with undertaking a discrete unit of operations.

Figure 7.1 *Operations Plan*

- Operations strategy
- Scope of operations
- Ongoing operations

Lazybones has the interesting opportunity to generate negative working capital. That is, Lazybones may collect payments before it has to pay the cost of delivering the service. Depending on revenue ramp-up this could be a significant competitive advantage because Lazybones can use the deposits to partially fund the growth of a store (e.g., adding new washing machines and dryers as demand increases). In any case, entrepreneurs have to understand the implications of operating strategy on cash management.

Another factor that has cash implications is whether your operations strategy is to "buy" or to "build" the production process. Lazybones is using a combination of buy and build. For the company-owned stores, Lazybones builds the stores, meaning that it finances and operates each of the company-owned stores. On the other hand, Lazybones franchise strategy is equivalent to a buy strategy in that each franchise pays a royalty to carry the Lazybones brand and use its proprietary operations system. How do you make the decision of whether to buy or build? First, what is the nature of your competitive advantage? Reflect again on your competitive advantages and concentrate your efforts on what you do best. Outsource other requirements. Apple has a sophisticated mix of buy and build. Their distribution channel is particularly complex, using a rapidly growing branded store system and a series of distributors, especially campus bookstores. You might also build if your advantage lies in some proprietary technology that you need to keep close control of (although you may only need to make the component where your technology is embedded). Lazybones is building company-owned stores to demonstrate to potential franchises how the system works and to provide proof that its system will generate profits for the franchisees. If building isn't central to your competitive advantage, consider buying, which means outsourcing the operations, because the second key factor to keep in mind for this decision is the cost. Building often means huge fixed expenditures up front, which means raising more capital, diluting your own equity, and lengthening the time to breakeven. Basically it means increased risk.

Operations Strategy

The first subsection provides a strategy overview. How does your business win/compare on the dimensions of cost, quality, timeliness, and flexibility? The emphasis should be on those aspects that provide your venture with a comparative advantage. Lazybones has perfected an efficient operation over years of refinement that allow it to clean tons of laundry and make sure it is delivered to the right people at a lower cost than its competition.

It is also appropriate to discuss geographic location of production facilities and how this enhances the firm's competitive advantage. Proximate location to large universities is central to the Lazybones business model. Discuss available labor, local regulations, transportation, infrastructure, and proximity to suppliers. The section should also provide a description of the facilities, how the facilities will be acquired (bought or leased), and how future growth will be handled (e.g., renting an adjoining building, etc.).

Scope of Operations

What is the production process for your product or service? A diagram powerfully illustrates how your company adds value to the various inputs. Constructing the diagram also facilitates the decision of which production aspects to keep in house (build) and which to outsource (buy). Considering that cash flow is king and that resource-constrained new ventures should typically minimize fixed expenses on production facilities, the general rule is to outsource as much production as possible. However, as already discussed, there is a major caveat to that rule. Your venture should control aspects of production that are central to your competitive advantage. Outsourcing the aspects that aren't proprietary reduces fixed cost for production equipment and facility expenditures, which means that you have to raise less money and give up less equity. As with most things in entrepreneurship, over time you will revisit this question.

The scope of operations should also discuss partnerships with vendors, suppliers, and partners. Again, the diagram should illustrate the supplier and vendor relationships by category (or by name if the list isn't too long and you have already identified your suppliers). The diagram helps you visualize the various relationships and ways to better manage or eliminate them. The operations diagram also helps entrepreneurs to identify personnel needs. For example, the diagram provides an indication of how many production workers might be needed, dependent upon the hours of operations, number of shifts, and so forth.

Ongoing Operations

This section builds upon the scope of operations by providing details on day-to-day activities. For example, how many units will be produced in a day and what kinds of inputs are necessary? An operating cycle overview diagram graphically illustrates the impact of production on cash flow. As entrepreneurs complete this detail, they can start to establish performance parameters, which will help monitor and modify the production process into the future and test assumptions regarding competitive advantages. If this is an operational business plan, the level of detail may include specific job descriptions, but for the typical business plan, this level of detail would be much more than an investor, for example, would need or want to see in the initial evaluation phase.

Lazybones Operations Plan

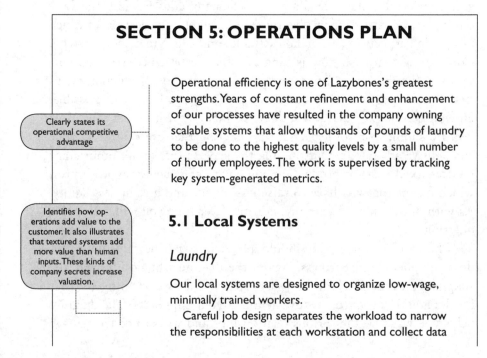

SECTION 5: OPERATIONS PLAN

Clearly states its operational competitive advantage

Operational efficiency is one of Lazybones's greatest strengths. Years of constant refinement and enhancement of our processes have resulted in the company owning scalable systems that allow thousands of pounds of laundry to be done to the highest quality levels by a small number of hourly employees. The work is supervised by tracking key system-generated metrics.

Identifies how operations add value to the customer. It also illustrates that textured systems add more value than human inputs. These kinds of company secrets increase valuation.

5.1 Local Systems

Laundry

Our local systems are designed to organize low-wage, minimally trained workers.

Careful job design separates the workload to narrow the responsibilities at each workstation and collect data on performance measurement. This improves customer service and allows us to track down complaints.

Exhibit 5.1   *Sample Laundry Package Label*

> This visual catch point quickly illustrates tracking and control of laundry, a central element to the Lazybones competitive advantage.

Reid Harris

100 Magazine Street
MIT 99 Bay State Rd on Thursday
Pound Limit:
Pounds this week: 17.6
Washed By Martha ~ Folded By Edith ~ Packaged By John

DELIVERY CODE

(D1)16700

4 Items Air Dried
these items are air-dried for 60 minutes to remove as much moisture as possible then folded and packaged separately even if still damp.

2 Items Sent for Dry Cleaning
Dry Cleaning is done at a separate facility and will be delivered back in approx 3 days.

LOAD CODE

WECARE@LAZYBONES.NET
1.877.215.2105

- Pickup and Delivery: Our drivers use simple handheld bar-code readers to track their pickups, loads, and deliveries. A Global Positioning System (GPS) is onboard our vehicles to track driver location in real time and reconstruct routes in the event of mistakes.
- Weighing In: Laundry bags are weighed in to the hundredth of a pound. Weigh person as well as date and time are collected. Untagged bags are bar-coded.
- Washing: Data is collected as laundry is put into the wash, including wash person, date and time, any special requests, dry clean items, and which machines laundry is washed and dried in.
- Folding: We track which folders folded which customer's laundry when, and the pounds folded per hour for each employee, so that quality and error rates can be tracked to individual employees. Folder names are displayed on completed package labels.
- Packaging: Finished laundry is precisely weighed and discrepancies are checked. Folding and washing quality and accuracy of special request completions are checked off. Wrap person, date, and times are logged.
- Video Surveillance: Each workstation on the laundry floor is video recorded for quality assurance. Live video and playback are accessible over the Internet.

Storage

- Pickup and Delivery: Two man teams pick up storage directly from student dorm rooms and apartments. Handheld scanners collect item codes and counts as well as pickup times. Customers are given handwritten carbon lists of items picked up. On delivery, package codes are scanned and the manifest is signed.
- Invoicing: Trucks are unloaded in our warehouse; items are separated by customer and logged in by type and size. Items are inventoried, palletized, wrapped, and stored. Item descriptions, charges, insured values, and resting locations are posted to customer accounts, and fully itemized receipts are issued.

> The plan does a nice job of detailing the scope of the operational process. Dan could have added a timeline to show how long this process takes.

> Since storage is a central part of the Lazybones business, the operations around it are also detailed.

> The detail in this section helps the reader understand this is a sophisticated business.

Exhibit 5.2   *Storage Items Put Away for the Summer*

> Strategically placing a few pictures throughout the plan helps communicate the business and also draws the reader's attention.

5.2 Centralized Systems

A number of key Lazybones operational functions are performed at corporate headquarters (HQ). This includes the company Web site, customer databases, and a customer call center. These can be performed more efficiently from a central location, and keeping them centralized allows franchisees and store managers to focus on the quality and efficiency of their staff and services on campus. It also allows Lazybones to select managers and franchisees that lack experience with higher-level business operations but have the work ethic to successfully run a facility.

> The centralized strategy will allow Lazybones to scale. Each component of the centralized systems should provide economies of scale and robust competitive advantage that increases with system growth.

Web Site

The Lazybones Web site will be the primary means for customers to sign up for laundry delivery and get information about the company's services. It includes pricing tables, forms for delivery sign-up (including credit card payments), make complaints, and find FAQs with answers to typical customer questions and concerns. The Web site will specifically address key issues that have proven to escalate the activity-based costs of customers and their parents: scheduling of pickups, confirming these schedules, and tracking their progress in real time. Laundry status is live-updated as it transitions from wash to fold to delivery. Parents and students can also access storage status, insured

> Today, every business needs a Web site. Many companies use a Web site as a form of advertising who they are and what they do. Lazybones goes further in that the Web site is part of the customer interaction experience. Like many e-retailers, customers can buy and track their service through the Lazybones Web site.

values, shipping dates, and tracking numbers. Additionally, our Web site can solicit and aggregate customer surveys about quality, efficiency, and overall satisfaction, to be factored into staff evaluations. These surveys also allow customers to register complaints about local managers and franchise owners, keeping HQ informed about local operations. GPS trackers onboard the delivery vans provide real-time locations to the customer-service personnel to allow for accurate timeframes for pickups and deliveries. Eventually, the locations of the vans will also be available to customers in real time via the Web site.

> For a service-oriented business, managing customer complaints and questions is central to success. While many companies today use automated call centers or direct you to the Web site, Lazybones enhances its competitive advantage by providing access to a live person. There are costs associated with such a service, so it is important to make sure that the benefit (satisfied customers who continue to do business with you) outweighs the cost.

Call Center

Customers can also sign up for laundry service via our toll-free number. This customer service phone bank is able to handle all customer questions, concerns, and complaints. Customer service personnel coordinate with personnel at a location to address problems, such as lost or damaged laundry, and track such issues until they are resolved.

Databases

> Database development and management are key components of scale and essential in franchise operations.

Lazybones HQ maintains a customized Web-based database of all customers, account histories, personnel hours, and laundry processes. This automates much of the data collection and generates the forms, e-mails, and reports needed. The system automates credit card charging so that a customer's account is charged as their laundry is weighed in, and the company can automatically solicit renewal if the customer's plan is running out. These hundreds of weekly invoices and payments are automatically posted in batches into QuickBooks accounting files for each location.

> This section highlights how corporate operational activities provide value to the franchise. This will likely motivate potential franchisees to buy a Lazybones franchise.

5.3 Franchise Operational Differences

Customer Service

Company-owned stores use the call center to handle customer service. Franchisees will not be required to use the call center, but can pay to use it when short staffed or extra busy. All local customer service complaint and issue e-mails come directly to the local franchise, who must then handle and resolve them.

Payroll and Accounting

Corporate HQ handles state and federal taxes for its company-owned stores. Franchisees will have to process their own sales taxes and their own annual returns. Child support, workers' comp, and disability insurance are all handled by HQ for owned stores but will be handled locally by franchisees.

Services Offered

Company-owned stores offer laundry, dry cleaning, and storage services on campus. We will mandate that franchisees offer these core services, but we have experience with and will support several additional services for students, including but not limited to: bottled water, maid service, packing, and shipping. We will also remain open to suggestions from franchisees for additional services to offer.

> Although a franchise, Lazybones is allowing its franchisees to add services that they think will bring in incremental revenue. Based upon the experience of the franchisees, Lazybones may add successful services to the nationwide system.

5.4 Facilities and Equipment

Local

> Identifies geographic location and criteria for store sites

Locally, Lazybones can use inexpensive, industrial-quality space since there is no need for an attractive storefront. For storage we rent temporary warehouse space within 60 minutes' driving time of campus at discounted rates. We generally rent two warehouses, a smaller one for belongings of students going abroad in spring semester, and a larger one for the summer (Exhibit 5.3).

Exhibit 5.3 *Local Leases*

Leases	Monthly	No. Months	Annual
Laundry building	$3,000	12	$36,000
Storage warehouse 1	$750	6	$4,500
Storage warehouse 1	$3,500	4	$14,000
Van lease	$350	12	$4,200
Annual lease total			$58,700

Equipment for a new Lazybones, including washers, dryers, bar-code scanners, computers, and digital video equipment, will be leased whenever possible (Exhibit 5.4). Continental-Girbau has leased laundry equipment to all our locations and indicated a willingness to finance the full cost of this equipment and its installation in return for being our exclusive laundry equipment supplier.

> Table nicely captures basic rental costs for a unit. This table when aggregated across units feeds the pro forma financials. Breaking costs by operation and activity helps entrepreneurs develop more realistic and accurate projections. Locations can scale as business dictates by adding space (and costs).

Again, detailed costs by activity help you develop accurate projections. **Exhibit 5.4** *Start-up Equipment Costs*

Equipment	Quantity	Price	Total
20 lb washers	6	$2,500	$15,000
35 lb washers	2	$3,500	$7,000
30 lb dryers	6	$1,500	$9,000
50 lb dryers	2	$2,250	$4,500
Air-dry dryers	2	$250	$500
Detergent dispensers	8	$200	$1,600
Water heater and softener	2	$1,500	$3,000
Plumbing and install	1	$15,000	$15,000
Total laundry equipment			$55,600
Computers and networking	4	$500	$2,000
Scanners and swipers	5	$200	$1,000
Miscellaneous equipment	1	$1,000	$1,000
Video equipment	1	$1,500	$1,500
Laundry supplies	1	$1,000	$1,000
Upfront van	1	$1,000	$1,000
Upfront rent	2	$1,500	$3,000
Upfront salaries	2	$2,000	$4,000
Marketing blitz	1	$10,000	$10,000
Travel	1	$2,500	$2,500
Total office and other			$27,000
Total start-up costs			$82,600

A franchise has the same location and equipment needs as a company store. We will provide a facility guideline to a franchisee so they can find and rent suitable space. Continental-Girbau has already indicated their likely support of $1 mm in franchise-assignable financing.

5.5 Staffing Plan

Excluding hourly staff, Lazybones company stores will employ eight location managers and one call center manager. Lazybones HQ will reorganize itself to change from managing locations to servicing franchise customers. The Lazybones HQ staff will consist of executive managers and a single administrative assistant until the company opens its first franchises. Additional staff will be added as the number of franchisees increases (Exhibits 5.5 and 5.6). This will include a marketing manager to advertise for and find franchisees; a financial analyst to monitor franchisees' books and guide them in keeping those books; operations consultants to help franchisees set up and improve their operations; a quality consultant to monitor customer satisfaction and ensure franchisees are meeting quality standards; and information technology staff to keep the databases and other hardware and software running, including offering tech support with key operational systems to Lazybones stores and franchises.

> The headcount table is useful because it not only shows how much each person or position will be paid, but also when these people will be hired. This table also helps Dan build accurate projections because it feeds directly into his pro formas.

Exhibit 5.5 *HQ Staffing Plan by Year*[2]

	Year 1	Year 2	Year 3	Year 4	Year 5
No. franchises	0	5	15	35	60
CEO	$60,000	$60,000	$70,000	$80,000	$90,000
COO	$60,000	$60,000	$70,000	$80,000	$90,000
CDO	$60,000	$60,000	$70,000	$80,000	$90,000
Operations consultants				$65,000	$130,000
Marketing managers				$65,000	$65,000
Financial analysts			$65,000	$65,000	$130,000
Quality consultants		$50,000	$50,000	$50,000	$100,000
Information technology staff		$55,000	$55,000	$55,000	$110,000
Administrative assistants		$30,000	$30,000	$30,000	$60,000
	$180,000	$315,000	$410,000	$570,000	$865,000

Exhibit 5.6 *Lazybones Organizational Chart*

> The organization chart is useful to show the flow of information and responsibility. Considering this is a franchise operation, one gap on the team might be a director of franchisee training.

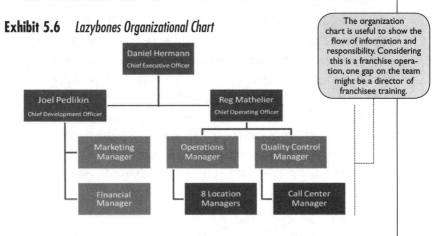

---

[2]CEO = chief executive officer, COO = chief operating officer, CDO = chief development officer

Development Plan

The development plan highlights the process of preparing the company for generating sales and provides a detailed timeline. Figure 7.2 highlights the main sections of the development plan. Many new ventures will require a significant level of effort and time to launch the product or service. This section tells how the business will progress from its current position to a going concern. For example, new software or hardware products often require months of development. For a retail business plan, site location, financing, and zoning can take 12–18 months or longer. The development plan should detail the steps taken to get to that developed software product.

Development Strategy

What work remains to be completed? What factors need to come together for development to be successful? What risks to development does the firm face? For example, software development is notorious for taking longer and costing more than most companies originally imagined. Detailing the necessary work and what is required for the work to be considered successful helps entrepreneurs to understand and manage the risks involved. After you have laid out these details, a development timeline is assembled.

Development Timeline

A development timeline is a schedule that highlights major milestones and can be used to monitor progress and make changes. The timeline helps entrepreneurs track major events and schedule activities to best execute on those events. It also provides a guidepost of promised accomplishments for your investors. Because Lazybones is developing a business format franchise, a detailed timeline creates a detailed understanding of the unit of operations (store) and then describe the process of replicating these stores. Therefore, the business plan should illustrate the number of stores that will open and the timeline to achieve those openings.

Figure 7.2 *Development Plan*

- Development strategy
- Development timeline

Lazybones Development Plan

SECTION 6: DEVELOPMENT PLAN

Our five-year goals for Lazybones are as follows:

> This is a bit of a hedge. The entrepreneurs might consider the following: "To achieve X number of stores to create a national network of branded operations with economies of scale and market leadership." Being specific adds credibility to the plan

- To provide high-quality services to U.S. college students. While we expect these services to be laundry and storage, we may provide additional services as well.
- To reach sufficient revenue levels and a sufficient number of franchises that potential acquirers see it as an established, solid business.
- To grow the company to the point where its net income can easily support the three principal executives into the foreseeable future.

The Lazybones development timeline has been crafted to meet these goals. It begins with opening four new company stores over the first year. During that first year we create a detailed franchising plan, culminating in the sale and opening of the first franchises at the beginning of year two. Additional franchises are opened in January, May, or September of each subsequent year. Lazybones plans to have eight company stores and 60 franchises within five years.

> Although Lazybones isn't seeking outside capital, the last bullet point raises a red flag for investors. This statement doesn't prioritize my investment as the priority, but the principals' well-being.

Exhibit 6.1 *Development Timeline*

Parameters	Year 1	Year 2	Year 3	Year 4	Year 5
Number of new owned locations	4	0	0	0	0
Total number of owned locations	8	8	8	8	8
Number of new franchised locations	0	5	10	20	25
Total number of franchised locations	0	5	15	35	60
Franchise fee	$35,000	$35,000	$35,000	$35,000	$35,000
Franchise revenue %	7	7	7	7	7

> Most timelines are represented as Gantt charts, which allow finer-grained detailing of necessary activities. This timeline is rather limited in what it communicates. The last two lines are not adding any new information other than to say that the franchise fee and royalty will remain the same throughout the period. As such, they can be eliminated.

Opening of Owned Stores

Opening company stores first is a critical element in our plan. This will test the business model in eight total locations, giving potential franchisees confidence that the model works in a variety of environments. These stores will also provide much of the cash flow required for getting into the franchise business. Furthermore, we project that after five years, the eight company stores will provide sufficient net income to satisfy the second of our primary goals.

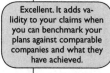

They have set up a conflict of interest that is common in franchising but most folks work hard to avoid it. They are explicitly stating the company-owned stores are more important than the franchises. In a business plan, never put forth that one of your primary goals is to personally benefit. It isn't necessary to say; it is expected and implied.

In other words, even if our franchising plan does not meet its targets, the company stores alone suffice to meet one of our key development goals.

Opening of Franchises

A more detailed Gantt chart timeline could itemize each of these activities, who would be responsible for leading them, and when the activities would start (e.g., beginning month) and end (e.g., ending month).

During year one, we will also be planning our move into franchising. This will require hiring franchise consultants and lawyers and working with them to create our franchising plan, Franchise Disclosure Document (FDD), and other documents required to meet federal and state franchising regulations.

The franchising plan will include a detailed franchise marketing plan and prepared marketing and advertising materials. Most of this work will be completed halfway through year one, and we will begin actively advertising for and seeking out franchisees.

Obtaining a good return on this franchising investment will require selling many franchises. The planned rate of expansion is summarized in Exhibit 6.1. While this is an aggressive plan, we have identified five other personal services franchise businesses that grew substantially faster, as shown in Exhibit 6.2.

Excellent. It adds validity to your claims when you can benchmark your plans against comparable companies and what they have achieved.

Exhibit 6.2 *Other Competitors' Franchise Growth Rates*

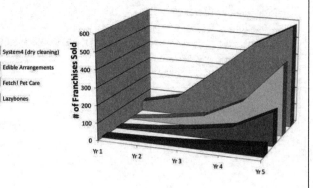

Expansion

To date, all company stores have been opened in July and begun servicing customers at the start of the fall semester in September. This has been based on our belief that the start of a new school year is the optimal time to sign up customers. However, it would be extremely difficult for our organization to support rapid growth if all new franchises must be opened simultaneously. Therefore, we intend to test different opening dates for these four company stores: three in July 2009, and one in January 2010. We will choose six potential locations for the additional three company stores by May 2009.

> A Gantt chart would capture the timing of these activities.

We will then perform detailed investigations of the potential sites, investigating the demographics of all nearby colleges, contacting the administrations of those schools to assess their willingness to sign cooperative agreements, identifying specific facility locations and facility costs near the schools of interest, and determining whether we have any known qualified candidates to open and manage the locations. We will down-select to three specific company store locations by July 2009.

Chapter Summary

Although the operations and development plans tend to be shorter in the standard business plan format, these sections deserve attention and will be considerably longer if you are writing an operational business plan for internal use. Also, as illustrated by Lazybones, service organizations tend to have more detailed operations plans because they are able to outsource less of their business. The activities covered in these sections have direct cost implications. The more homework you do, the better you will be able to plan your cash flow. This has direct implications on the amount of capital you will need to raise and on how you make strategic decisions once you launch. Even if you are outsourcing most of the production of your product, you need to spend the time understanding the operational process so that you can evaluate and chose the most appropriate partner. Making a bad decision on a production partner will have potentially large cost and time implications. So make sure you have the deep understanding needed.

The development plan is also an important exercise. Planning all the details needed to successfully launch a business is imperative to success. In Chapter 2, we provided you with the Business Planning Guide, which is basically a template for you to lay out all the actions that you need to take. As you go through the marketing plan and the operations plan, you should be able to fill in more details that need to happen during your launch phase. Tim DeMello, serial founder of Wall Street Games and Streamline, shared with students when he visited Babson College a useful exercise that he uses to identify all the necessary actions that need to be taken. Tim had every member of his founding team sit in a room with flip chart sheets taped to the walls. The team members then went around the room writing down actions. In a second cycle they added detailed actions that supported the major actions identified in the first round. They continued in this manner until they exhausted new action items. Then the actions were organized along a timeline, and responsibilities were given to the appropriate team members. Although we don't recommend showing that level of detail in your development timeline, the deep learning that you gain by going through the process will be invaluable and will help you make sound decisions going forward.

8 TEAM: THE KEY TO SUCCESS

Georges Doriot, the father of venture capital and founder of American Research and Development Corporation (the first modern-day venture capital firm), said that he would rather "back an 'A' entrepreneur with a 'B' idea than a 'B' entrepreneur with an 'A' idea." He reasoned that an A team could more easily mold and reshape a B idea into a winning opportunity than a B team could execute on an A idea. Therefore, the team section of the business plan is often the section that professional investors read after the executive summary. Thus it is critical that the plan depict the members responsible for key activities and convey that they are exceptional people with integrity, knowledge, and skills.

In many cases, the business planning process will help you identify what gaps exist on your team. It is rare that a founding entrepreneur has all the competencies needed to launch a successful business. In fact, research suggests that ventures launched by teams are more likely to become sustainable businesses than those launched by individuals. One study found that over 83 percent of companies that achieved sales of $5 million or more were started by teams, whereas just over half of the companies launched by teams failed.[1] So as you complete different sections of the plan, especially the marketing, operations and development plans, start thinking of what kind of skills you need to successfully execute on those activities. For example, we work with many bright engineers who understand technology and how to create sophisticated devices or software, yet they lack the business skills necessary to launch a viable business, such as business development, sales, or finance. We also work

---

[1] Jeffry Timmons and Susam Skinner, "The Route 128 One Hundred," working paper, Wellesley, MA: Babson College, 1984.

with lots of really sharp businesspeople who have identified a customer need but don't have the technology background to build a prototype. In these situations, it makes sense to recruit a cofounder—someone who complements your skill set so that together you can fill the gaps on the team.

However, you can't fill out a complete team right from the beginning. It would drain too much cash (assuming you paid them), and it would dilute too much equity. You need to be strategic and think about the two to five key people you will need to succeed. You also have to anticipate when you will need them. If we look at Lazybones, Dan and Reg ran the company and its first two units for 15 years. Now, as they contemplate growth, they've attracted Joel to help move the company to the next level. The core team forms the nucleus that can achieve several key milestones. As the milestones are met and surpassed, you start building out your infrastructure, which means hiring more people.

When building your core founding team, identify people that can multitask and are willing to take on lots of duties. Although individuals with extensive experience can be valuable additions, if their experience has been with large corporations they may have difficulty adjusting to the start-up mentality. The corporate person may expect all the administrative support provided by the previous company, as well as the ability to narrowly focus on a given area of specialization. This can create a culture clash because in the start-up environment, team members need to wear many hats. They need to help others in areas that may not be their areas of expertise. They have to accomplish tasks with minimal administrative support (don't waste resources on administrative support too early in the launch phase). Although there are many other considerations when building your team, keeping in mind the foregoing advice will help you launch your business and conserve resources.

Considering how important the team is to your company's success, you need to present the power of the team as effectively as possible. We suggest that you have an introductory paragraph that talks about how the team came together. The subsequent subsections will provide the detail that connects the teams skills with the requirements of the opportunity.

Team Bios and Roles

It is best to start by identifying the founding team members and their titles. Often, the lead entrepreneur assumes a CEO role. However, if you are young and have limited business experience, it is usually more productive to state that the company will seek a qualified CEO as it grows. In these cases, the lead entrepreneur may assume a chief technology officer (CTO) role (if this person develops the technology), vice resident of business development, or even founder. However, don't let these options confine you. The key is to convince investors that you have assembled the best team possible and that your team can execute on the brilliant concept you are proposing.

Once responsibilities and titles have been defined, names and a short bio should be filled in. The bios should demonstrate records of success. If you have previously started a business (even if it failed), highlight the company's accomplishments. If you have no previous entrepreneurial experience, discuss your achievements within your last job. For example, bios often contain a description of the number of people the entrepreneur previously managed and, more importantly, a measure of economic success, such as growing division sales by 20-plus percent. Developing a top line, managing to a bottom line, and creating stakeholder value are the components of experience you want to highlight. The bio should also demonstrate your leadership capabilities. To complement this description, résumés are often included as an appendix.

Advisory Boards, Board of Directors, Strategic Partners, External Members

To enhance the team's credentials, many entrepreneurs find that they are more attractive to investors if they have strong advisory boards. In building an advisory board, identify individuals with relevant experience within your industry who can help you achieve important milestones, and also think about whether these people will invest. For example, Lazybones has achieved several milestones (opening two more company stores to complement the two original ones) and has targeted other milestones in the future (opening four additional company stores and then franchising). While Dan and Reg have proven the concept, franchising is a new strategy for the team. Thus, they may seek advisers with franchising experience. Industry experts provide legitimacy to your new business as well as strong technical advice. Other advisory board members may bring other skills, such as financial, legal, or management expertise. Thus, it is common to see lawyers, professors, and accountants, among others, who can assist the venture's growth on advisory boards. Moreover, if your firm has a strategic supplier or key customer, it may make sense to invite that person onto your advisory board. Typically, these individuals are remunerated with a small equity stake and compensation for any organized meetings. The key in building your advisory board is to identify the most important needs and the milestones your organization will face during its launch phase.

By law, most organization types require a board of directors. This is different than an advisory board (although board directors can also provide the needed expertise). The primary role of the board of directors is to oversee the company on behalf of the investors. This fiduciary duty carries legal rights, obligations, and liabilities. As we have seen with the demise of large corporations such as Enron, AIG, and others, board directors may be sued if a corporation fails and shareholders believe the board members did not exert sufficient oversight of company officers. Sometimes a key industry expert will be willing to join the company as an adviser but not as a director because of these liability issues, but also because being a board director implies a long-term commitment to the company. Potential board members may not be willing to give the extra time that board directorship suggests. In any case, the business plan needs to briefly describe the size of the board, its role within the organization, and any current board members. Most major investors, such as venture capitalists, will require one or more board seats. Usually, the lead entrepreneur and one or more inside company members (e.g., chief financial officers, vice presidents, etc.) will also have board seats. At its present stage of development, the Lazybones board consists of insiders. If it seeks and secures outside equity infusions, investors will likely take board seats as well.

Strategic partners may not necessarily be on your advisory board or your board of directors, but they still provide credibility to your venture. In such cases, it makes sense to highlight their involvement in your company's success. It is also common to list external team members, such as the law firm and accounting firm that your venture uses. The key in this section is to demonstrate that your firm can successfully execute the concept. A strong team provides the foundation that conveys your venture will implement the opportunity successfully.

Compensation and Ownership

A capstone to the team section should be a table containing key team members by role, compensation, and ownership equity. A brief description of the table should explain why the compensation is appropriate. Many entrepreneurs choose not to pay themselves in the early months. Although this strategy conserves cash flow, it would misrepresent the individual's worth to the organization. Therefore, the table should contain what salary the employee is due, and then if deemed necessary that salary can be deferred until a time when cash flow is strong. Another column, which can be powerful, shows what the person's current or most recent compensation was and what she will be paid in the new company. We are most impressed when we see highly qualified entrepreneurs taking a smaller salary than at their previous job. It suggests that the entrepreneur really believes in the upside payoff the company's growth will generate. Of course, the entrepreneur plans on increasing this salary as the venture grows and starts to thrive. As such, the description of the schedule should underscore the plan to increase salaries in the future. It is also a good idea to hold stock aside for future key hires and establish a stock option pool for lower-level but critical employees, such as software engineers. It is not uncommon to see a management set-aside of 15 percent of the company in addition to any that equity team members may buy. Again, the plan should discuss such provisions. Let's take a look at the Lazybones team section.

Lazybones Management Team Plan

SECTION 7: THE TEAM

Management Plan

The growth trajectory laid out in this plan will introduce significant management challenges to the company. Our rapid growth will demand that each new store, both owned and franchised, require little unanticipated week-to-week support. We will depend on managers and franchisees to do much of the local problem solving on their own, so we need strong leadership from Human Resources in finding and hiring these people.

Our information technology (IT) systems need to be reliable and stable as we grow, and there is a significant Web component to our plans both operationally and marketing-wise. As we embark on an aggressive growth plan, we have added Joel Pedlikin, who has 10 years of leadership

> Nicely lays out what the company needs in management talent. Although it appears that the team is overlooking a gap on the leadership team. As noted in the previous chapter, some high-level person to oversee training is imperative.

> The expert IT system will need to scale as the company grows. Thus Lazybones should be thinking about who and when they might bring in a CTO-level person.

experience with larger companies. Joel provides the valuable experience of running larger companies, which will help us improve our ability to predict the workloads and sales demand.

Both Joel and founder Dan Hermann are finishing the Babson MBA program now. Babson has accepted Lazybones into its Entrepreneurship Intensity Track program and connected the two with a mentor, Jim Bardis, who has extensive franchise experience.

In addition to Jim, the Lazybones team intends to seek out a four-person board of advisers to support the company's leadership.

Dan Hermann

Dan will be the company's president. Dan will have overall responsibility for managing the company and will be the final decision maker on all major corporate issues. However, on a day-to-day basis he will focus on strategic planning, marketing, and brand building. He soon will have a Babson MBA to go with his 15 years of experience managing and growing Lazybones.

> Shows how the newest top management team member fills a gap in Lazybones. They may want to be more explicit that Joel will be responsible for the development and management of integrated operating systems as the company experiences rapid growth. While Joel has experience in larger companies, the plan needs to clearly state how this experience is applicable to a growing Lazybones.

> Suggests that Lazybones has an important mentor. Currently the team is lacking franchising experience, and, since this is central to their growth strategy, it may be a good addition to the top management team. We would like to see more about who Jim is and his accomplishments.

> A board of advisers can be a powerful tool to help Dan shape his strategy, identify gaps and weaknesses in the company and team, and network to other needed resources. Once the board of advisers is in place, a brief bio of each member will further validate the power of the Lazybones team.

> A picture of each founder is a visual catchpoint that will draw reader to this very important section of the plan.

> Identify role and responsibilities for each team member. We would like to see the bio reiterate what Dan has done to date with Lazybones.

Reg Mathelier

Reg will be Lazybones's chief operating officer and vice president. He will take primary responsibility for the company's day-to-day operations, focusing on the company stores. His responsibilities will include leading all administrative and accounting management. This is consistent with Reg's successful role at Lazybones for the last 15 years.

Joel Pedlikin

Joel will be Lazybones's chief development officer and vice president. He will focus on planning and implementing the company's five-year growth plan and will lead all franchising efforts. Joel has 10 years of executive experience at companies with revenues between $12 million and $50 million a year, two engineering degrees from Brown and Caltech, and a Babson MBA on the way.

> We would like to see this expanded so we can gauge how this experience directly translates to success for Lazybones. For instance, was Joel responsible for driving growth at his previous companies?

> This section could end with a compensation table and breakdown of founder equity. However, it has been removed from this book to protect confidentiality for Lazybones.

Chapter Summary

The team section is critical to successfully selling your vision. You need to build a team that adds credibility. This may be difficult for younger entrepreneurs or those who are entering into a field where they have less experience. If you find that your team section isn't compelling, you probably need to add a key member or two to your core team. Your ability to build a strong team is your first market test. If you can convince others of the attractiveness of the opportunity, you've passed a major milestone that will make your company more attractive to investors and other stakeholders.

9

THE CRITICAL RISKS AND OFFERING PLAN SECTIONS

Critical Risks: Understanding the Critical Drivers to Your Success

Every company faces a number of risks that may threaten its survival. The risks are enhanced for new ventures. Although the business plan, to this point, is creating a story of success, there are a number of threats that readers will identify and recognize. As such, the plan needs to acknowledge these potential risks, otherwise investors will believe that the entrepreneur is naive or untrustworthy and may possibly withhold investment. It is also important for you to understand these critical risks because they most often are directly related to assumptions that will drive your venture's success or failure. For example, a common critical risk is market acceptance. Will your target customers really buy your product in the quantity and price you expect? If they do, then your top line revenue projections will likely hold true, but if not, your business could be in serious trouble. How should you present these critical risks without scaring your investor, or for that matter, so that you feel comfortable proceeding with the venture? Identify the risk and then state your contingency plan. For instance, if your primary target customer doesn't buy your product as expected, a contingency might be to redirect your efforts toward a new customer group. Critical assumptions vary from one company to another, but some

127

common categories are market interest and growth potential, competitor actions and retaliation, time and cost of development, operating expenses, and availability and timing of financing. We will briefly highlight these major categories, but don't limit your thinking to only these categories. Try to anticipate what else may be important for your company.

Market Interest and Growth Potential

The biggest risk any new venture faces is that once the product is developed, sales fall short of expectations. Although there are a number of things that can be done to minimize this risk, such as market research, focus groups, and beta sites, it is difficult to gauge overall demand and growth of that demand until your product hits the market. This risk must be stated, but countered with the tactics and contingencies the company will undertake if problems develop. For example, sales risk can be reduced by hiring an experienced sales executive, developing an effective advertising and marketing plan, or identifying not only a primary target customer but also secondary and tertiary target customers that the company will seek if the primary customer proves less interested.

Perhaps the most effective method of countering this risk is to test the market in a series of iterations. Thus many technology companies go through alpha and beta testing. Basically, alpha testing is having "an insider" group test the product. This can be as sophisticated as focus groups, university MBA classes, and industry experts, or as simple as your employees and friends. They report back and you make modifications so that the product better meets their needs. Next, you might move the product to beta sites. Beta sites are a handful of selected customers who understand that the product is early stage and that there may be glitches, yet they are excited by the product's potential. Usually, you can get these customers to pay a minimal price for the product, but sometimes you let them use it at no charge. After you make adjustments during the beta stage, you start controlled roll-out to the broader market. Try to have feedback loops where you can learn from the customers and make changes so that the product is better in the next version. Although this strategy is commonly associated with technology products such as software, this strategy can work with all businesses.

Lazybones has basically mimicked the market test methodology. Its alpha site was the first store in Madison, Wisconsin. There, Dan and Reg learned how to sell their laundry service, collect dirty laundry from their clients, clean and package it, and return it. The company spent many years figuring out how to do this more efficiently. The beta site was the Syracuse location. Here, Dan learned whether they could replicate the model to another geographical location (would Syracuse students react and use the service in a similar way as Wisconsin students?). Adding more company stores in Boston and Boulder was another test to see whether they could hire managers to run those locations with oversight from a centralized headquarters. The next step, and the one that the current plan focuses on, is how to implement a franchising program to rapidly grow the business. The moral of the lesson is that you can preserve resources by incrementally testing your business concept rather than building an entire franchise network at the outset.

Competitor Actions and Retaliation

Having the opportunity to work with entrepreneurs and student entre-preneurs over the years, we have always been struck by the firmly held belief that either direct competition didn't exist, or it was sleepy and slow to react. There have been some cases where this is indeed true, but we caution against using it as a key assumption of your venture's success. Most entrepreneurs passionately believe that they are offering something new and wonderful that is clearly different from what is currently being offered. They go on to state that existing competition won't attack their niche in the near future, oftentimes because the competition is a large company concerned only with the larger market. The implicit assumption is that your smaller niche isn't as interesting to the competition because the potential profitability of the niche is lower than the broader market. The risk that this assessment is wrong should be acknowledged. One counter to this threat is that your venture has room in its gross margins, and cash available to withstand and fight back against such attacks. You should also identify some strategies to protect and reposition yourself should an attack occur. One of the authors' favorite entrepreneurs once said, "Never underestimate the vindictiveness of a competitor."

Time and Cost to Development

As mentioned in the development plan section, many factors can delay and add to the expense of developing your product. The business plan should identify the factors that may hinder progress and success. For instance, during the extended high-tech boom of the late nineties, there was an acute shortage of skilled software engineers. That led to the risk of hiring and retaining the most qualified professionals. One way to counter the problem might be to outsource some development to the underemployed engineers in India. Compensation, equity participation, flexible hours, and other benefits that the firm could offer might also minimize the risk.

Operating Expenses

Operating expenses have a way of growing beyond expectations. Sales and administration, marketing, and interest expenses are some of the areas that the entrepreneur needs to monitor and manage. The business plan should highlight how these expenses were forecasted (comparable companies and detailed analysis), but also talk about contingencies such as slowing the hiring of support personnel, especially if development or other key tasks take longer than expected.

Availability and Timing of Financing

We can't stress enough how important cash flow is to the survival and flourishing of a new venture. One major risk that most new ventures face is that they will have difficulty obtaining needed financing, both equity and debt. If the current business plan is meant to attract investors and is successful, that isn't a near-term risk, but most ventures will need follow-on financing. If the firm fails to make progress (or meet key milestones), it may not be able to secure additional financing on favorable terms. A contingency to this risk is to identify alternative sources that are viable or strategies to slow the "burn rate."[1] Less well known is beating projections exponentially and not being able to finance growth. One of the authors is currently working with a new venture that forged a new channel of distribution that will increase revenue 10-fold per month in the first year. They have only 30 days to get the financing to ramp up inventory by millions of dollars!

There are a number of other risks that might apply to your business. Acknowledge them and discuss how you can overcome them. Doing so generates confidence in your investors. Let's take a look at the Lazybones critical risk section.

---

[1]Burn rate is how much more cash the company is expending each month than earning in revenue.

Lazybones Critical Risk Section

SECTION 8: CRITICAL RISKS

- We assume that the Lazybones business model can be applied with minimal changes to a large number of campuses across the country.

  While this is based on years of experience at the University of Wisconsin, Syracuse University, Boston University, and the University of Colorado, the assumption may still prove flawed at some schools. We will carefully monitor customer acquisition rates on each new campus and franchise only after opening four more company stores.

> Replication risk

> Response is bolstered by the fact that the business model has been successfully replicated before. They also talk about a monitoring strategy to make sure that the new stores are on track. Metrics to measure progress are an important aspect of planning.

- We believe we offer franchisees a sufficiently attractive value proposition that they will remain franchisees even after they have learned all the details of how to successfully run a Lazybones.

  However, there is a risk that some of them will try to operate independently and compete with us once their franchise contracts are up. We address this risk by having franchisees sign noncompete agreements, insisting any university agreements be signed with Lazybones headquarters rather than the franchisee, and keeping many critical functions centrally controlled.

> Imitation risk. Will potential franchisees forgo Lazybones and try to start their own laundry service?

> Addresses this risk with a combination of legal remedies and providing critical services through headquarters. Lazybones might consider enlisting a prestigious law firm that specializes in franchise documents in their team section.

- Our financial plan assumes that all company stores and franchisees can grow at roughly the speed the Syracuse and Wisconsin Lazybones grew.

  Not achieving this growth would mean that new stores would operate longer at a loss, reducing the company's margins. We address this by placing strong, highly motivated managers in charge of each location and giving them both the authority to identify ways to grow and the experienced support of executive management.

> Customer acceptance risk

> Since Lazybones operations are fixed locations, it has plans to use more aggressive customer acquisition strategies to remedy any problems.

- We assume that the company can thrive and grow without a high-level executive possessing franchising experience.

  This is based on the success stories of other franchises whose executives were highly competent businesspeople but new to franchising. We will address this risk by creating an executive advisory council with experienced franchisers as members and enlisting experienced franchising consultants for additional support.

> Franchisee quality risk

> The experienced panel will help those new franchisees that need some mentoring. While advisory councils are a good start, Lazybones also needs to mitigate execution risk at the store level. They will need a field support program to help franchisees in trouble. This is a gap in the current plan.

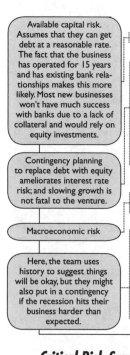

Available capital risk. Assumes that they can get debt at a reasonable rate. The fact that the business has operated for 15 years and has existing bank relationships makes this more likely. Most new businesses won't have much success with banks due to a lack of collateral and would rely on equity investments.

Contingency planning to replace debt with equity ameliorates interest rate risk; and slowing growth is not fatal to the venture.

Macroeconomic risk

Here, the team uses history to suggest things will be okay, but they might also put in a contingency if the recession hits their business harder than expected.

• Lazybones plans to borrow money to support its rapid growth.

We assume we can borrow this money from a combination of friends and family, Continental-Girbau, and other lenders for an interest rate of 9 percent or less with payback in five years. If this assumption proves wrong, we may need to seek out equity investors, pay a higher interest rate, or, worst case, slow Lazybones's growth to a rate that can be supported via the cash flow from our existing company stores.

• We assume that the state of the U.S. economy will not adversely affect Lazybones.

Specifically we believe that we will still be able to sign up customers at roughly the same rate we have sustained over the last 15 years. While the current recession promises to be larger than any economic slowdown experienced over this period, our experience has shown that the company's growth is not correlated to the state of the economy.

Critical Risk Summary

As you review the Lazybones critical risk section, note that Dan raises the risk and then discusses how the company is managing the risk. What other risks do you think Dan has overlooked? Do you believe he has adequately countered those risks? What other contingencies might improve his chances of success if some of these risks come into play? The key is to anticipate what might happen and prepare to manage those risks if they do arise. Role playing with your mentors and friends can be a valuable exercise in preparing this section.

Offering Plan: How Much Do You Need?

As we stated in Chapter 1, one of the main reasons to write a business plan is to seek and secure financing. It is important for entrepreneurs to identify not only how much capital they are seeking, but also how they will use that funding to achieve milestones. A "sources and uses" table effectively articulates your needs. The sources section details how much capital the entrepreneur needs and the types of financing such as equity investment and debt infusions. The uses section details how the money will be spent. Typically, the entrepreneur should secure enough financing to last 12 to 18 months, but whatever the period you are funding there should be a value creation milestone that can be achieved with each tranche of investment. Taking more capital means that the entrepreneur gives up more equity. In other words, taking more capital than you need dilutes your ownership share. Taking less means that the entrepreneur may run out of cash before reaching milestones that equate to higher valuations.

It is important to think of financing as happening over time. You want to raise enough capital during each stage to reach a critical milestone, and then go out and raise additional capital to hit the next milestone. This round financing strategy preserves your equity because you give up equity based upon the perceived value of the company at the time of financing. When you are first starting out, you may only have a concept, no product. The value of that concept (and therefore the company) is relatively lower than the value will be when you have a physical product that is a manifestation of the concept. Likewise, the company that has a physical product but little or no sales is valued less than a company that has sales. If, at the time you start your company, you raise all the capital you need to penetrate the market and reach a certain sales level (cash flow positive), you would likely have to give away most of the equity because the value of the company is so low in the beginning. On the other hand, if you manage the financing over time, you will give up less equity in total.

Most entrepreneurs have difficulty determining how much of the company they must give to investors at each stage of financing (i.e., their company's valuation). The reality is that valuation is always a negotiation between you and your investors. With that understanding, a company's valuation is based upon what it has accomplished to date, or, said differently, what milestones it has achieved. A company that is prelaunch (just a concept) is worth very little. Lazybones, with a proven concept and several operating units, has risen dramatically in value. Developing a product increases the value. Achieving sales increases the value further. So how might you gauge the value of your company at this stage? One technique that is relatively simple and robust is the venture capital technique. Don't worry, you don't need to be seeking venture capital to use it.

The technique basically looks at what return an investor needs to achieve and then looks at the company's potential to generate that return. Lazybones is seeking debt so we do not need to value the company, but what if they decide they need to use equity. Dan is seeking $500,000 to finance the next four company stores. Considering that the company has four successful operating units and a 15-year history, investors would gauge the likelihood that they will get their investment back plus an attractive rate of return. The rate of return that an investor might expect would be around 20 percent per year. Why? This investment isn't risk free. Even though Lazybones has been successful to date, many companies going through rapid expansion overextend and end in bankruptcy. For example, Bennigan's, a casual dining franchise, went into bankruptcy shortly after the 2008 recession began. A combination of lots of competition in the casual dining arena (e.g., Chili's, Applebees, and so on) along with declining interest in dining out due to the recession pushed the franchisor over the brink. Could something like this happen to Lazybones? The probability is low but not zero, and even if the company is not technically bankrupt, they may not be in a position to fund the debt service to investors. Thus there is a risk premium associated with this investment. When an investor puts money into a start-up firm, it is privately held. That means there is no market for investors to sell their shares. Thus investors expect to hold their shares for many years until the company either (1) goes public, (2) is acquired by another firm, or (3) generates enough cash flow and profit to buy back the investors' shares. Let's assume that investors expect to get their money out of the company in five years:

Investment (i) = $500,000.
Length of investment (n) = five years.
Expected Rate of Return = 20 percent.
We are seeking the future value (FV) of the investment.

$FV = i(1 + ROR)^n.$
$FV = \$500,000 (1 + .20)^5.$
$FV = \$1,244,160.$

Now that we know the future value of the investment, we need to determine the future value of the company. We need to estimate the company's profit after tax in the future and then multiply that figure by a price earnings ratio. In this case, I'm just using the projections that Lazybones presents in its plan for year five.

Lazybones's profit after tax (PAT) = $2.1 million.
Consumer services price earnings ratio (PE)[2] = 10.

---

[2]From Yahoo/Finance for Consumer Services Industry, www.biz.yahoo.com/p/762conameu.html, accessed August 15, 2010.

FV = PAT * PE.
FV = $2.1 million * 10.
FV = $21 million.

The final step is to divide the FV of the investment by the FV of the company. What we are basically doing is determining what percentage of the company the investors need to own so that they can earn their expected rate of return.

FVi/FV company
$1.2 million/$21 million = 5.7 percent.

Once we know how much equity Lazybones needs to sell in order to secure the investment, we can determine the value of Lazybones today (rather than in five years). We basically divide the investment sought ($500,000) by the equity that amount purchases (5.7 percent).
$500,000/5.7 percent = $8.75 million.
As investors, we are always skeptical of an entrepreneur's projections. Entrepreneurs tend to be overly optimistic. Thus you need to be careful when going through this exercise not to be surprised if an investor has a significantly different estimate than you do. There are several assumptions that can be widely off. Based upon our extensive experience, for instance, we would demand 10 percent of Lazybones's equity. That percentage suggests that Lazybones is worth roughly $5 million today ($500,000/10 percent). We are, in essence, questioning the accuracy of Dan's financial projections. We are basically questioning whether all the new units that Lazybones opens will perform as well as the established units. Thus we expect revenues to be lower than Dan projects.
Even though we recommend you have some basis for determining how much equity you need to give in order to secure the investment, we do not suggest that you present that in the business plan. This gets back to our opening statement that valuation is a negotiation. As such, putting in how much you are willing to give might end the negotiation before it starts. If, for instance, we saw that Lazybones only wants to relinquish 5.7 percent of its equity for $500,000, we would probably not consider the investment. Nonetheless, it is important for you to go through this exercise so that you are operating from a position of knowledge when you do negotiate with investors. Thus the offering section is often very short, possibly only a sources and uses table with some description around it. Let's look at the Lazybones offering plan.

Lazybones Offering Plan

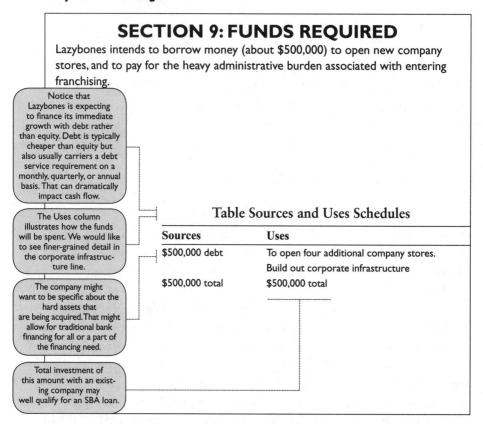

SECTION 9: FUNDS REQUIRED

Lazybones intends to borrow money (about $500,000) to open new company stores, and to pay for the heavy administrative burden associated with entering franchising.

Notice that Lazybones is expecting to finance its immediate growth with debt rather than equity. Debt is typically cheaper than equity but also usually carriers a debt service requirement on a monthly, quarterly, or annual basis. That can dramatically impact cash flow.

The Uses column illustrates how the funds will be spent. We would like to see finer-grained detail in the corporate infrastructure line.

The company might want to be specific about the hard assets that are being acquired. That might allow for traditional bank financing for all or a part of the financing need.

Total investment of this amount with an existing company may well qualify for an SBA loan.

Table Sources and Uses Schedules

Sources	Uses
$500,000 debt	To open four additional company stores.
	Build out corporate infrastructure
$500,000 total	$500,000 total

Chapter Summary

In this chapter, we have focused on the critical assumptions that drive your venture's success and also the offering plan. Both of these elements are influenced by your pro forma projections. Your critical assumptions are often directly related to revenue and cost projections that we will see on your income statement. Your offering valuation is also derived from your income statement projections. The next chapter will examine how to develop sound financial projections.

10 FINANCIAL PLAN: TELLING YOUR STORY IN NUMBERS

Much of your business plan is your verbal and graphic description of the opportunity and how you will execute it. The financial plan is the mathematical equivalent. The growth in revenues speaks to the upside of your opportunity. The expenses indicate how much it costs to deliver the product or service. Cash flow statements serve as an early warning system to potential problems (or critical risks), and the balance sheet represents the resources required to put the delivery system into place. That being said, generating realistic financials is one of the most intimidating hurdles that many entrepreneurs face. There is a temptation to hire an accountant to create your financials for you. Big mistake. Although painful, the deep learning that you acquire by struggling through the numbers helps you really understand your business. Always remember that the numbers in the financial statements are a reflection of the actions you take in your business. You learn what actions drive revenue and costs. You learn how cash flow can go negative even if you are growing and profitable. Besides, you will be presenting your plan to investors and bankers. You lose credibility if you can't explain the numbers yourself.

This chapter will provide you a broad overview of how to generate realistic financials. We will highlight a dual-strategy approach to building your model: comparable analysis and the buildup technique.

Entrepreneurs should do both approaches, and, with work and skill, the two approaches allow entrepreneurs to paint a textured picture of the financial structure of their new venture.

Creating Initial Estimates

Comparable Method .

Entrepreneurs are notoriously optimistic in their projections. One phrase that entrepreneurs overuse in their business plan, especially the financial plan, is "conservative estimate." History proves that 99 percent of all entrepreneurs are amazingly aggressive in their projections. Professional investors recognize this problem and often discount financials up to 50 percent from the entrepreneur's projections. Such action greatly impacts the valuation of your company and means that you will have to give up more equity for the needed financing. How do you prevent this unhappy surprise from happening? Validate your projections by comparing your firm's pro forma financials to existing firms' actual performance. If you can convince investors that your projections are reasonable and refer to existing companies as a basis for your beliefs, you will get a valuation closer to what you expected. Obviously, no two firms are exactly alike, and if you were to launch an online bookstore, it would be unlikely that your firm would perfectly mirror Amazon.com. However, the comparable method doesn't mean that you substitute another firm's financials for your own; it means that you use that as a starting point. Early in this process variances will emerge that require analysis and explanation. Some of the variances will highlight your competitive advantages; others will be red flags marking weaknesses. Many of the variances may be explained by the stage of your company's development. New ventures go through a learning process, which translates into less efficient use of resources early on (higher expenses). You need to understand why the differences exist.

The first step is to start with your benchmark company's common-sized income statement through the use of percentages for all line items. With the revenue line equaling 100 percent, work your way down the income statement and express each line (e.g., cost of goods sold, gross margin, etc.) as a percentage of revenue. We use year five projections for Lazybones because the early years tend to be more volatile due to rapid growth. We have identified two good comparables for Lazybones. The first is ServiceMaster. It is a larger franchisor that is the umbrella organization for such service brands as Merry Maids and Terminex. Since they are in the space of providing services, including housecleaning, to the end user, it seems to be a good match. We also looked at Yum Brands, the franchisor of such name brand fast food restaurants as KFC, Taco Bell, and Pizza Hut, among others. Exhibit 10.1 shows Lazybones, Service-Master, and Yum Brands side by side. We can see that the Lazybones gross margin is 37 percent and 51 percent higher than ServiceMaster and Yum Brands, respectively. ServiceMaster, like Lazybones, provides services to its end customers through a combination of company-owned stores and franchisees. Its costs of goods sold (COGS) may be higher because the services are often provided at the customer's location. Lawn services have to happen at the customer's lawn. Pest control has to happen at the customer's place of residence or business. Thus they may need considerably more people to conduct the services. Considering that Yum Brands operates a number of restaurants, their COGS includes food and direct labor, whereas Lazybones only has direct labor and minimal expenses for detergent and other cleaning products. Thus the higher gross margin may make sense, but the magnitude would cause us to take a closer look to make sure that we aren't neglecting some major cost items.

The large difference in gross margins translates to larger earnings before interest, taxes, depreciation, and amortization (EBITDA) margins, even though Lazybones is expecting to spend more on sales, general, and administrative (SG&A) costs. One last area of analysis might be sales per employee. We counted 14 corporate employees per Lazybones headcount chart, and we assumed four full-time equivalents for each of the eight company-owned stores. In this situation, Lazybones falls between the two comparable companies in sales per employee. This suggests that Lazybones is likely in the right range for the number of employees they are projecting.

Remember, gross variance, positive or negative, from the comparable companies will draw investor attention and *should* draw your attention. If you understand these discrepancies, you can address investor concerns with confidence, increasing your credibility. If we were potential investors in Lazybones, we would want Dan to clearly articulate how he can manage such impressive margins. While we understand that his company-owned stores are likely to perform similarly to the existing units in Madison and Syracuse, we wonder if he has accurately captured the costs and margins of being a franchisor. We would expect that the franchised units might dampen margins while the company is putting franchisor support overhead in place, although this strategy has the benefit of enabling rapid expansion at a relatively lower cost.

Exhibit 10.1   Lazybones Common Sized Income Statement with Industry Comparable

	Service Master 2009		Yum Brands 2009		Lazybones Year 5		Service Master Variance	Yum Brands Variance
	(000)		(000)					
Revenue	$3,240,079	100%	$10,836,000	100%	$7,843,381	100%	0%	0%
COGS	$1,913,329	59%	$7,934,000	73%	$1,747,125	22%	-37%	-51%
GM	$1,326,750	41%	$2,902,000	27%	$6,096,256	78%	37%	51%
SG&A	$852,831	26%	$1,209,000	11%	$2,588,839	33%	7%	22%
Other OpEx	$54,876	2%	$103,000	1%		0%	-2%	-1%
EBITDA	$419,043	13%	$1,590,000	15%	$3,507,417	45%	32%	30%
Employees	27,000		49,000		46			
Sales/Employee	$120		$221		$171		$51	$-50

Individual company benchmarks are a good foundation to build upon, but we would also look at industry averages. The RMA, Capital IQ, and other databases are an excellent source to use as starting points in building financial statements relevant to your industry. Check to see if your local library subscribes to these databases or others that provide industry information. Secondary sources often break down the industries by firm size. For example, smaller firms have different common-sized percentages than do larger firms. Thus these sources help entrepreneurs build income statements by providing industry averages for costs of goods sold, salary expenses, interest expenses, and so forth. Again, your firm will differ from these industry averages, but you should be able to explain why your firm differs.

Build-Up Method

The second method is the build-up method. This approach derives from the scientific finding that people make better decisions by decomposing the problem into smaller parts. For financial pro forma construction, this is relatively easy. The place to start is the income statement. Identify all of your revenue sources (usually, the various product offerings). Instead of visualizing what you will sell in a month or a year, break it down to the day. For example, if you are starting a new restaurant, you should estimate how many customers you might serve in a particular day and how much they would spend per visit based upon the types of meals and beverages they would buy. In essence, you are developing an average ticket price per customer. Then multiply that by the number of days of operation in the year. Once you have the typical day, you can make adjustments due to cyclical aspects of the business, such as day parts, slow days, or slow months. You could then multiply your estimates if you were to open up a chain of restaurants. Once you have gone through a couple of iterations of each approach, you should be able to reconcile the differences.

One schedule that is particularly powerful in building up your cost estimates is a headcount schedule. In Chapter 7, we saw the headcount table for Lazybones. Next assign average salaries to these employees and then funnel them into the appropriate income statement lines. We must also remember that employees cost more than just their salaries and wages. You will have to pay employment taxes (social security, etc.), possibly health insurance, workers' compensation, retirement, and any other benefits you wish to provide. This is sometimes called the labor burden, and, as such, we multiply salary times a burden rate. Twenty-eight percent is usually a good first estimate. Breaking down to this level of detail enables entrepreneurs to more accurately aggregate up to their real headcount expenses, which tend to be the major line item in most companies.

The Financial Statements

Going through the preceding exercises allows you to construct a "realistic" set of pro forma financials. The financial statements that must be included in your plan are the income statement, cash flow statement, and balance sheet. Investors typically expect five years of financials, recognizing that the farther out one goes, the less accurate the forecasts are. The rationale behind five years is that the first two years show the firm surviving, and the last three years show the upside growth potential. The majority of new ventures lose money for the first two years. Therefore, the income statement and cash flow statement should be month to month during the first two years to show how much cash is needed until the firm can become self-sustaining. Month-to-month analysis shows cash flow decreasing and provides an early warning system as to when the entrepreneur should seek the next round of financing. Years three through five only need to be illustrated on an annual basis as this communicates your vision for growth, and a textured understanding of the forces that you believe will drive the future of the business. The balance sheet can be on an annual basis for all five years since it is reporting a snapshot on the last day of a particular period, but it will inform the investor of the magnitude of the resources you expect to marshal to fulfill your vision.

The key to constructing the actual financials is building the statements on a spreadsheet and linking the different financial statements together. This can be difficult, but Frank Moyes and Steve Lawrence at the University of Colorado have developed an excellent Excel template that you can download from their Web site.[1]

Description of Statements

Once the financial spreadsheets are completed, you should write a description preceding each statement explaining the key drivers impacting the numbers. Although you understand all the assumptions and comparables that went into building the financial forecast, the reader needs the background spelled out. The explanation should have four subheadings: overview, income statement, cash flow, and balance sheet. The overview section should highlight the major assumptions that drive your revenue and expenses. This section should map to several of the critical risks you identified earlier. The income statement description goes into more detail as to some of the revenue and cost drivers that haven't been discussed in the overview section. The cash flow description talks about the timing of cash infusions, accounts payable, accounts receivable, and so forth. The balance sheet description illustrates how major ratios change as the firm grows. For instance, talk about the inventory turn ratio. How long do you hold inventory before it is sold? This conversion has a major impact on your company's cash position, because holding inventory means that cash is tied up. Let's examine the Lazybones financial plan.

---

[1] As of the writing of this chapter, you could download the template at www.leeds-faculty.colorado.edu/moyes/html/resources.htm. Hit the hotlink: Financial Projections Model v6.8.9.

Lazybones Financial Plan

Section 10: Financials

The development plan outlined in Section 6 will result in dramatic increases in Lazybones's financial performance. In five years we expect:

> The first major section provides a high-level overview of the major assumptions that drive the projections.

- Annual revenue increase of 6×
- Annual net profit increase of 10×
- Annual cash flow increases of 5×

We will accomplish this by opening four new company stores and 60 new franchises on the timeline shown in Exhibit 6.1.

Summaries of Lazybones's present actual financials and five-year projected financials are shown in Exhibit 10.2.

> Notice how Dan refers back to other portions of the plan where he detailed growth. Putting in exhibits throughout the plan helps you build stronger financial projections.

Exhibit 10.2 Five-Year Projected Financials

	Revenue	Gross Profit	Net Profit	Total Assets
Present actual	$1.2M	$0.7M	$0.2M	$0.2M
Five-year projected	$7.1M	$5.5M	$2.0M	$3.5M

Company stores will contribute all local income and expenses, franchise locations will contribute upfront franchise fees and a percentage of revenue (additional contributions such as call center fees are considered to be negligible and are not built into this model). Our operations and financial plans are based on an academic year, split into two semesters: the fall semester (July to December) and spring semester (January to June). Both company stores and franchises are opened and begin producing revenue in May, July, or January of a given year.

10.1 Revenue Drivers

> This section starts to explain what drives the income sheet. For a franchise, sound store model economics are an important building block.

Revenues for established company stores, new company stores, future company stores, and franchises are all predicted off of a model (the "model store") created from historic data from our mature Wisconsin and Syracuse locations.

These models are built up from the historic numbers of new customers per semester for both laundry and storage and average revenue per customer for both laundry and storage. This allows

> Notice that since Lazybones has a 15-year operating history, their comparable is the performance of the first two stores. Many of you reading this book are starting companies from scratch. In this case, center your discussion around how your business is similar to or different from industry averages or a benchmark company.

Note that this is also a critical risk that Dan discussed in the previous critical risk section of the plan.

the model to include annual increases in service prices. We make the critical assumption that sales growth on all new company stores and franchises will basically follow the growth curve experienced at existing locations.

Essentially, we are assuming that local managers and franchisees will be able to perform at least as well as the company's founders did, because they will have access to all the systems developed and lessons learned over the last 15 years and are motivated entrepreneurs. History has shown that franchisees typically perform at about the same revenue levels of company stores but *outperform* company stores on the bottom line.[2]

Established Company Stores (Syracuse and Madison)

Red flag word. Basically same as "conservative." Don't need this adjective.

We generally advise that you provide an explanation as to why revenues will continue to grow. In the Lazybones case, it could be a function of growing their client base or raising prices. In either event, 10 percent increases can't go on forever. At some point, the stores would reach their capacity and either have to expand or open a second location within that city.

These locations' year one revenues are their actual revenues from 2007 adjusted up by 20 percent. This 20 percent increase is a cautious extrapolation from the actual Syracuse and Madison revenues as of October 2008. The revenues at these two locations are then assumed to increase by 10 percent each subsequent year of the financial plan.

New Company Stores (Boston, Boulder)

We have created a five-year income (revenue and cost) model (the model store) for all new Lazybones locations based on Syracuse's and Madison's historical numbers. Since both Boston and Boulder will have been in business for a full year by Fall 2009, their "first-year" revenue contributions to the financial plan are based on the "second-year" numbers of this model store. In other words, Boston and Boulder are treated as new locations that have already been open a full year in "year one."

Be careful not to complicate the analysis and get diverted from the key message. In this case, the Lazybones message is that the model is sound and can be scaled to a national brand.

Future Company Stores

The same model used for the foregoing new company stores' revenues is used for all future company stores (i.e., company stores opened in year one or later of the development plan). The correlation between model store year and financial

---

[2] S. Spinelli, R. Rosenberg, and S. Birley, "Franchising: Pathway to Wealth Creation," 2001. http://www.amazon.com/s/?ie=UTF8&keywords=pathway+to+wealth+creation&tag=googhydr-20&index=stripbooks&hvadid=340138075l&ref=pd_sl_4ljsplooy6_b

plan year is simple: Year one of the model contributes to the year of their opening on the financial plan, year two of the model contributes to the year after they were added to the financial plan, and so forth.

> Dan is talking about company stores and what a model store looks like. However, Lazybones gets revenues from both company stores and franchise fees.

Franchises

Each franchise contributes revenue to Lazybones in two ways: an initial start-up franchise fee of $35,000 and 7 percent of their annual revenues. Each franchise also contributes 1 percent of their revenue to an advertising fund, but since this fund is separate from all other corporate operations, it is not visible in the financial plan.

Exhibit 10.3   Corporate Revenue

Overview					
Month	**Year 1**	**Year 2**	**Year 3**	**Year 4**	**Year 5**
Revenue					
Total number of owned stores	8	8	8	8	8
Total number of franchises	0	5	15	35	60
Owned stores					
SU and UW growth rate	120%	112%	109%	106%	103%
Syracuse					
Laundry	$433,880	$485,945	$529,681	$577,352	$629,313
Storage	$219,241	$245,550	$267,650	$291.738	$317,995
Syracuse total	$653,121	$731,495	$797,331	$869,090	$947,308
Wisconsin					
Laundry	$330,910	$370,619	$403,975	$440,333	$479,963
Storage	$275,731	$308,819	$336,613	$366,908	$399,929
Wisconsin total	$606,641	$679,438	$740,558	$807,241	$879,892
Boston	$204,392	$371,440	$532,752	$709,266	$730,544
Colorado	$204,392	$371,440	$532,752	$709,266	$730,544
Additional owned stores	$364,631	$817,567	$1,485,760	$2,131,007	$2,837,065
Owned store contribution	$2,033,177	$2,971,381	$4,120,687	$5,225,870	$6,125,353
Franchises					
Franchise fees	$0	$175,000	$350,000	$700,000	$8175,00
Franchise %	$0	$31,905	$135,348	$400,699	$892,146
Franchise contribution	$0	$206,905	$485,348	$1,100,699	$1,767,146
Total revenue	$2,033,177	$3,178,286	$4,574,531	$6,326,569	$7,891,599

> Notice how this table breaks down the different revenue lines. We see both laundry and storage for the Syracuse and Wisconsin stores and then store totals for the new company-owned stores based upon historic performance. Finally, the franchise totals are shown. At the top of the table, they list the revenue drivers (number of company-owned stores and franchises by year). They also show projected growth rate of the existing Syracuse and Wisconsin stores (note 120 percent means that it will grow 20 percent more than the previous year). As we noted above, we'd prefer to see an explanation of that growth rate to further enhance the accuracy of the projection. Breaking the revenues down by this level of detail helps create more accurate projections.

10.2 Cost Drivers

Company Store Start-Up Costs

Based on recent experience with Boulder and Boston, we estimate new location start-up costs at $82,600 (Exhibit 5.4).

Franchisees must obtain these funds for a franchise. Lazybones intends to borrow this money for company stores. Laundry equipment and installation for Boston and Boulder were financed through the manufacturer Continental-Girbau, and computer equipment through Dell.

The costs of opening additional company stores will also be financed through Continental-Girbau. We have confirmed this supplier's willingness to finance the entire $82,600 per store in return for being Lazybones's equipment supplier. Based on previous experience, we assume this money will be loaned at 9 percent interest over five years.

This contributes between $7,000 (year one) and $3,000 (year five) per year in interest expense per store depending on which year of operations they are in.

Company Store Variable Costs

Both the variable (cost of goods sold, COGS) and operating expenses of the company stores are based on the same historical models described earlier. Variable costs (COGS) are calculated as a percentage of laundry revenue, storage revenue, or both, depending on which type of revenue the costs contribute. For instance, laundry supplies only contribute to laundry revenue, and truck rentals only contribute to storage revenue.

By far the largest cost at Lazybones facilities is labor. Hourly employees, who do not receive benefits and only work when school is in session, perform most of the labor (laundry washing, folding, and delivery). This labor is treated as a variable cost proportional to workload.

Exhibit 10.4 Owned Store COGS Breakdown by Percent

Variable Cost Breakdown

Cost of Goods Sold	Laundry %	Storage %	Overall %
Dry cleaning	4.2		2.6
Laundry supplies	3.0		1.8
Payroll (COGS)	25.9	9.9	19.6
Bulking commissions	3.9	2.4	3.3
Storage supplies		1.4	0.5
Shipping		4.4	1.7
Truck rentals		6.0	2.4
Utilities	5.0		3.0
Payroll tax expenses	5.1	1.0	3.5
Merchant services	2.7	1.8	2.3
Discount services	0.1	0.2	3.5
Total COGS	49.9	27.1	44.2

> We like how, after Dan explains a portion of the model (i.e., costs), he has a table that breaks down the cost elements. Again, decomposing the business model into smaller parts helps you generate more accurate financials.

Operating Expenses

Managers' salaries, which do not vary based on workload, are separated under operating expenses. The next largest location cost is rent. Since the business can use inexpensive "industrial" space, Lazybones rents are lower than those for typical franchise businesses. The rents also vary tremendously by location. To be cautious, we have based our model store's rent on the most expensive of our four locations, Boston.

> Again, avoid adjectives like conservative or cautious. Entrepreneurs seldom are cautious in their projections. However, we like that he has chosen the highest cost location as his base model.

We have also included a factor increase of 5 percent per year to offset expense escalations (Exhibit 10.5).

Again, we like that Dan shows this level of detail. Some investors will focus on microanalysis and ask questions of these expenses. These questions may be nitpicking or they may be probes to test an entrepreneur's knowledge. For example, "What is your experience with 'customer damage' and what systems have you developed to minimize those losses?"

Exhibit 10.5   Model Store Operating Expenses

Annual Overhead	Year 1	Year 2	Year 3	Year 4	Year 5
Factor increase		1.05	1.05	1.05	1.05
Expenses					
Advertising expense	$15,000	$15,750	$16,538	$17,364	$18,233
Customer damages	$2,500	$3,908	$5,664	$7,782	$9,644
Automobile expense	$6,600	$6,930	$7,277	$7,640	$8,022
Total insurance	$13,003	$13,653	$14,336	$15,053	$15,805
Total interest expense	$7,074	$6,241	$5,331	$4,335	$3,246
Postage and delivery	$710	$746	$783	$822	$863
Total professional fees	$2,000	$2,100	$2,205	$2,315	$2,431
Primary rent	$36,000	$37,800	$39,690	$41,675	$43,758
Secondary rent	$4,500	$4,725	$4,961	$5,209	$5,470
Tertiary rent	$14,000	$14,700	$15,435	$16,207	$17,017
Repairs	$1,036	$1,088	$1,142	$1,199	$1,259
Telephone	$3,600	$3,780	$3,969	$4,167	$4,376
Internet	$2,113	$2,219	$2,330	$2,446	$2,568
Travel and entertainment	$500	$525	$551	$579	$608
Office supplies	$2,000	$2,100	$2,205	$2,315	$2,431
Administrative wages	$45,000	$47,250	$49,613	$52,093	$54,698
Customer service wages	$7,255	$7,618	$7,999	$8,399	$8,818
Total expense	$162,891	$171,133	$180,029	$189,600	$199,247

Think about how you label sections. "Corporate Headquarters Costs" screams overhead. "Centralized Store Support" says scale and competitive advantage. We would retitle this section. As we have noted throughout, it appears that Dan is overlooking the cost of supporting his franchisees.

Adding expert references gives your estimates credibility.

Corporate Headquarters Costs

Headquarters costs are dominated by professional fees and administrative labor. The $150,000 in professional fees in years one and two pay lawyers and consultants to create franchise agreements and the Franchise Disclosure Document. This estimate came from two sources: discussions with Babson professor Leslie Charm, an experienced franchiser, and the book *So You Want to Franchise Your Business* by Kestenbaum and Genn.

Professional fees in subsequent years are for updating these documents and dealing with franchise disputes. The administrative labor includes base salaries for executives; marketing, financial, and quality consultants; and administrative assistants. Executive base salaries are quite low, $60,000/year, with the expectation that they will earn equity and bonuses paid out of net income as the company succeeds. The number of each nonexecutive personnel grows according to a rough plan as the company adds franchises (Exhibit 6.1). Finally, to offset inflation and other normal cost increases, we assumed all other HQ expenses increase by 5 percent each year (Exhibit 10.6).

> Lazybones has both company stores and corporate headquarters to oversee. They need to detail them as separate cost centers. Furthermore, we see some gaps. No training cost? No marketing administration cost? No national contracts effort? Remember to explicitly delineate the costs associated with the competitive advantages you profess.

Exhibit 10.6 Headquarters Costs

Annual Overhead	Year 1	Year 2	Year 3	Year 4	Year 5
Factor increase		1.05	1.05	1.05	1.05
Expenses					
Advertising expense	$15,000	$100,000	$105,000	$110,250	$115,763
Insurance	$13,003	$13,653	$14,336	$15,053	$15,805
Interest expense	$0	$0	$0	$0	$0
Postage and delivery	$710	$746	$783	$822	$863
Professional fees	$50,000	$100,000	$50,000	$25,000	$25,000
Rent	$18,000	$18,900	$19,845	$20,837	$21,879
Telephone	$3,600	$3,780	$3,969	$4,167	$4,376
Internet	$2,113	$2,219	$2,330	$2,446	$2,568
Travel and entertainment	$500	$525	$551	$579	$608
Office supplies	$2,000	$2,100	$2,205	$2,315	$2,431
Administrative wages	$195,000	$315,000	$445,000	$530,000	$775,000
Total expense	$299,926	$556,926	$644,019	$711,469	$964,293

10.3 Income Statement

Exhibit 10.7 Five-Year Income Statement (detailed for first 18 months)

After laying out all the revenue and cost drivers, show the income sheet for five years, breaking out the first two years by month. As you look at the monthly projections you can see the seasonality in this business. Spikes at the beginning of each academic semester as new kids sign up for the service and then another spike in May for summer storage. Expect investors and debt providers to dissect and analyze the financials in great detail. They may also perform scenario analysis on these financials.

Part A: Year 1

	July	Aug	Sept	Oct	Nov	Dec	Semester	Jan	Feb	Mar	Apr	May	Jun	Semester	Year 1
Revenue															
Total number of owned stores	8						8							8	8
Total number of franchises	0						0							0	0
Syracuse total	$10,962	$54,350	$108,470	$21,694	$21,694	$43,618	$260,788	$108,470	$43,388	$23,886	$26,079	$179,548	$10,962	$392,333	$653,121
Wisconsin total	$13,787	$46,878	$82,728	$16,546	$16,546	$44,119	$220,601	$82,782	$33,091	$19,303	$22,060	$215,072	$13,787	$386,040	$606,641
Boston		$15,262	$38,141	$11,446	$7,631	$9,360	$81,854	$89,027	$5,087	$2,544	$4,623	$10,861	$10,397	$122,588	$204,392
Colorado		$15,262	$38,141	$11,446	$7,631	$9,360	$81,854	$89,027	$5,087	$2,544	$4,623	$10,861	$10,397	$122,588	$204,392
Additional owned stores		$11,628	$24,225	$31,977	$24,225	$25,968	$118,023	$145,350	$19,380	$9,690	$14,971	$30,813	$26,404	$246,608	$364,631
Owned store contribution	$24,749	$143,379	$291,731	$93,109	$77,726	$132,425	$763,120	$514,601	$106,033	$57,966	$72,356	$447,155	$71,946	$1,270,057	$2,033,177
Franchise															
Franchise fees															$0
Franchise %															$0
Franchise contribution															$0
Total revenue	$24,749	$143,379	$291,731	$93,109	$77,726	$132,425	$763,120	$514,601	$106,033	$57,966	$72,356	$447,155	$71,946	$1,270,057	$2,033,177
Owned stores COGS	$6,707	$65,903	$145,574	$46,461	$38,785	$47,450	$350,882	$256,786	$52,911	$27,797	$31,696	$133,267	$19,497	$521,954	$872,835
Total COGS	$6,707	$65,903	$145,574	$46,461	$38,785	$47,450	$350,882	$256,786	$52,911	$27,797	$31,696	$133,267	$19,497	$521,954	$872,835
Gross profit	$18,042	$77,476	$146,157	$46,648	$38,941	$84,975	$412,238	$257,815	$53,123	$30,170	$40,659	$313,888	$52,448	$748,104	$1,160,342
Gross profit %	73%	54%	50%	50%	50%	64%	54%	50%	50%	52%	56%	70%	73%	59%	57%
Expenses															
Owned store SG&A															
Syracuse	$17,710	$17,710	$17,710	$17,710	$17,710	$17,710	$106,261	$17,710	$17,710	$17,710	$17,710	$17,710	$17,710	$106,261	$212,523
Wisconsin	$18,117	$18,117	$18,117	$18,117	$18,117	$18,117	$108,705	$18,117	$18,117	$18,117	$18,117	$18,117	$18,117	$108,705	$217,410
Boston	$12,122	$12,122	$12,122	$12,122	$12,122	$12,122	$72,333	$12,122	$12,122	$12,122	$12,122	$12,122	$12,122	$72,333	$145,566
Colorado	$12,122	$12,122	$12,122	$12,122	$12,122	$12,122	$72,333	$12,122	$12,122	$12,122	$12,122	$12,122	$12,122	$72,333	$145,566
Additional owned stores	$59,722	$59,722	$52,722	$45,722	$45,722	$45,722	$312,634	$48,722	$48,722	$48,722	$55,722	$62,722	$59,722	$324,634	$637,268
Owned store SG&A	$119,844	$119,844	$112,844	$105,844	$105,844	$108,844	$673,066	$108,844	$108,844	$108,844	$115,844	$122,844	$119,844	$685,066	$1,358,133
Corporate SG&A	$27,359	$27,359	$27,359	$27,359	$27,359	$27,359	$164,157	$27,359	$27,359	$27,359	$27,359	$27,359	$27,359	$164,157	$328,314
EBITDA							($424,985)							($101,120)	($526,105)
Owned store taxes															$0
Corporate taxes															$0
Owned store interest	$3,541	$3,541	$3,541	$3,541	$3,541	$3,541	$21,244	$3,541	$3,541	$3,541	$3,541	$3,541	$3,541	$21,244	$42,849
Corporate interest	$2,500	$2,476	$2,452	$2,428	$2,403	$2,379	$14,637	$2,354	$2,329	$2,304	$2,279	$2,254	$2,229	$13,751	$28,388
Total expenses	$153,245	$153,221	$146,196	$139,172	$139,148	$142,123	$873,105	$142,099	$142,074	$142,049	$142,044	$155,999	$152,974	$884,218	$1,757,323
Net ordinary income	($135,203)	($75,745)	($39)	($92,524)	($100,207)	($57,148)	($460,886)	$115,717	($88,951)	($111,879)	($108,365)	$157,889	($100,525)	($136,115)	($596,981)
Net profit margin	-546%	-53%	0%	-99%	-129%	-43%	-60%	22%	-84%	-193%	-150%	35%	-140%	-11%	-29%

Exhibit 10.7: Five-Year Income Statement (detailed for first 18 months)

Part B: Years 2–5

> While it is common nomenclature to use parentheses to denote negative numbers, you may choose to use the negative sign and red font to make sure your reader doesn't overlook these important numbers.

	July	Aug	Sept	Oct	Nov	Dec	Semester	Jan	Feb	Mar	Apr	May	Jun	Semester 2	Year 2	Year 3	Year 4	Year 5
Revenue																		
Total number of owned stores	8						8	8						8	8	8	8	8
Total number of franchises	5						5	5						5	5	15	35	60
Syracuse total	$12,278	$60,872	$121,486	$24,297	$24,297	$48,852	$292,083	$121,486	$48,595	$26,753	$29,208	$201,093	$12,278	$439,413	$731,496	$797,331	$869,090	$947,308
Wisconsin total	$15,441	$52,503	$92,655	$18,531	$18,531	$49,413	$247,073	$92,655	$37,062	$21,619	$24,707	$240,881	$15,441	$432,365	$679,438	$740,588	$807,241	$879,892
Boston	$2,547	$34,597	$80,124	$16,025	$16,025	$21,119	$170,437	$80,124	$32,050	$16,534	$17,044	$52,704	$2,547	$201,003	$371,440	$532,752	$709,266	$730,544
Colorado	$2,547	$34,597	$80,124	$16,025	$16,025	$21,119	$170,437	$80,124	$32,050	$16,534	$17,044	$52,704	$2,547	$201,003	$371,440	$532,752	$709,266	$730,544
Additional owned stores	$0	$61,047	$152,618	$45,785	$30,524	$37,441	$327,414	$356,108	$20,349	$10,175	$18,492	$43,444	$41,586	$490,153	$817,567	$1,485,760	$2,131,007	$2,837,065
Owned store contribution	$32,813	$243,616	$527,007	$120,663	$105,401	$177,945	$1,207,445	$730,497	$170,105	$91,615	$106,495	$590,825	$74,399	$1,763,936	$2,971,381	$4,089,183	$5,225,870	$6,125,353
Franchises																		
Franchise fees	$175,000	$0	$0	$0	$0	$0	$175,000	$0	$0	$0	$0	$0	$0	$0	$175,000	$350,000	$700,000	$875,000
Franchise %	$0	$1,017	$2,120	$2,798	$2,120	$2,272	$10,327	$12,718	$1,696	$848	$1,310	$2,696	$2,310	$21,578	$31,905	$135,348	$400,699	$892,146
Franchise contribution	$175,000	$1,017	$2,120	$2,798	$2,120	$2,272	$185,327	$12,718	$1,696	$848	$1,310	$2,696	$2,310	$21,578	$206,905	$485,348	$1,100,699	$1,767,146
Total revenue	$207,813	$244,633	$529,127	$123,461	$107,521	$180,217	$1,392,772	$743,215	$171,801	$92,463	$107,805	$593,522	$76,709	$1,785,514	$3,178,286	$4,574,531	$6,326,569	$7,891,599
Owned stores COGS	$8,892	$114,083	$262,977	$60,211	$52,595	$68,775	$567,533	$364,518	$84,882	$44,220	$48,252	$179,506	$20,162	$741,540	$1,309,072	$1,296,739	$1,585,962	$1,747,125
Total COGS	$8,892	$114,083	$262,977	$60,211	$52,595	$68,775	$567,533	$364,518	$84,882	$44,220	$48,252	$179,506	$20,162	$741,540	$1,309,072	$1,296,739	$1,585,962	$1,747,125
Gross profit	$198,921	$130,550	$266,150	$63,250	$54,926	$111,442	$825,239	$378,697	$86,918	$48,243	$59,553	$414,016	$56,547	$1,043,975	$1,869,213	$3,277,792	$4,740,607	$6,144,474
Gross profit %	96%	53%	50%	51%	51%	62%	59%	51%	51%	52%	55%	70%	74%	58%	59%	72%	75%	78%
Expenses																		
Owned store SG&A																		
Syracuse	$19,835	$19,835	$19,835	$19,835	$19,835	$19,835	$119,013	$19,835	$19,835	$19,835	$19,835	$19,835	$19,835	$119,013	$238,026	$259,448	$275,015	$283,265
Wisconsin	$20,292	$20,292	$20,292	$20,292	$20,292	$20,292	$121,750	$20,292	$20,292	$20,292	$20,292	$20,292	$20,292	$121,750	$243,499	$265,414	$281,339	$289,779
Boston	$12,858	$12,858	$12,858	$12,858	$12,858	$12,858	$77,150	$12,858	$12,858	$12,858	$12,858	$12,858	$12,858	$77,150	$154,299	$163,849	$173,515	$178,721
Colorado	$12,858	$12,858	$12,858	$12,858	$12,858	$12,858	$77,150	$12,858	$12,858	$12,858	$12,858	$12,858	$12,858	$77,150	$154,299	$163,849	$173,515	$178,721
Additional owned stores	$48,489	$48,489	$48,489	$48,489	$48,489	$48,489	$290,932	$48,489	$48,489	$48,489	$48,489	$48,489	$48,489	$290,932	$581,864	$617,197	$655,396	$694,061
Owned store SG&A	$114,332	$114,332	$114,332	$114,332	$114,332	$114,332	$685,993	$114,332	$114,332	$114,332	$114,332	$114,332	$114,332	$685,993	$1,371,987	$1,469,757	$1,558,780	$1,624,546
Corporate SG&A	$28,727	$28,727	$28,727	$28,727	$28,727	$28,727	$172,365	$28,727	$28,727	$28,727	$28,727	$28,727	$28,727	$172,365	$344,730	$664,870	$728,201	$976,651
EBITDA	$55,862	($12,509)	$123,091	($79,809)	($88,133)	($31,617)	($33,119)	$235,638	($56,141)	($94,816)	($83,506)	$270,957	($86,512)	$185,616	$152,497	$1,143,165	$2,453,626	$3,543,277
Owned store taxes	$0	$0	$0	$0	$0	$14,520	$14,520	$0	$0	$0	$0	$0	$14,520	$14,520	$29,039	$69,401	$149,630	$210,164
Corporate taxes	$0	$0	$0	$0	$0	$25,924	$25,924	$0	$0	$0	$0	$0	$25,924	$25,924	$51,849	$399,387	$834,883	$1,188,320
Owned store interest	$3,129	$3,129	$3,129	$3,129	$3,129	$3,129	$18,772	$3,129	$3,129	$3,129	$3,129	$3,129	$3,129	$18,772	$37,543	$32,082	$26,045	$22,078
Corporate interest	$2,204	$2,178	$2,153	$2,127	$2,101	$2,075	$12,837	$2,049	$2,022	$1,996	$1,970	$1,943	$1,916	$11,896	$24,733	$20,852	$16,732	$12,358
Total expenses	$148,392	$148,366	$148,341	$148,315	$148,289	$188,707	$930,411	$148,237	$148,211	$148,184	$148,158	$148,131	$188,549	$929,470	$1,859,881	$2,656,350	$3,314,272	$4,034,117
Net ordinary income	$50,529	($17,816)	$117,809	($85,065)	($93,363)	($77,265)	($105,172)	$230,460	($61,292)	($99,941)	($88,605)	$265,885	($132,001)	$114,505	$9,333	$621,466	$1,426,336	$2,110,357
Net profit margin	24%	-7%	22%	-69%	-87%	-43%	-8%	31%	-36%	-108%	-82%	45%	-172%	6%	0%	14%	23%	27%

10.4 Balance Sheet

Exhibit 10.8 Five-Year Balance Sheet

	Pre-expansion	Year 1	Year 2	Year 3	Year 4	Year 5
Assets						
Current assets:						
Total cash and cash equivalents	$65,800	$138,173	$176,408	$852,623	$2,297,979	$4,402,628
Accounts receivable	$50,300	$1,000	$1,000	$1,000	$1,000	$1,000
Purchased inventories	$0					
Other current assets	$33,420	$33,420	$33,420	$33,420	$33,420	$33,420
Total current assets	$149,520	$172,593	$210,828	$887,043	$2,332,399	$4,437,048
Property plant and equipment	$142,400	$386,800	$386,800	$386,800	$386,800	$386,800
Less accumulated depreciation	-$92,320	-$181,280	-$270,240	-$359,200	-$448,160	-$537,120
Net property and equipment	$50,080	$205,520	$116,560	$27,600	-$61,360	-$150,320
Other assets						
Total assets	**$199,600**	**$378,113**	**$327,388**	**$914,643**	**$2,271,039**	**$4,286,728**
Liabilities and stockholders' equity						
Current liabilities:						
Accounts payable	$800	$800	$800	$800	$800	$800
Other current liabilities	$25,040	$25,040	$25,040	$25,040	$25,040	$25,040
Total current liabilities	$25,840	$25,840	$25,840	$25,840	$25,840	$25,840
Long-term debt		$775,494	$715,437	$649,746	$577,893	$531,443
Stockholders' equity:						
Common stock						
Additional paid capital						
Retained earnings		-$100,525	-$132,001	$652,945	$1,428,249	$2,062,139
Total stockholders' equity	$173,760	-$423,221	-$413,888	$239,057	$1,667,306	$3,729,445
Total liabilities and stockholders' equity	**$199,600**	**$378,113**	**$327,388**	**$914,643**	**$2,271,039**	**$4,286,728**

No regional offices/no fixed asset investment in franchise support. They might consider benchmarking the balance sheet to make sure they aren't missing important elements of their business model.

Notice how they explain the major categories within the balance sheet. Since this is primarily a cash/credit card business with low inventory, A/R, A/P, and inventory are relatively simple. However, if your business is a manufacturing business or carries inventory (like a retail store), your description of the balance sheet will need more detail

Lazybones's balance sheet (Exhibit 10.8) is simple, a reflection of the quality and simplicity of the business concept. This is a service business, so inventory is very small. Nearly all Lazybones customers pay upfront via credit card, so accounts receivable (A/R) is also very small. The exceptions are a few corporate laundry customers in Syracuse and Wisconsin who represent less than 5 percent of revenue and have never paid later than 40 days. Accounts payable is also fairly small, and since the company carries no A/R, Lazybones has easily paid its bills on time since the third year of its existence.

Significant investment is required in each location for laundry and other equipment (video cameras, bar code scanners, etc.). Historically, the company has been able to finance this equipment as well as its installation with the equipment manufacturer, Continental-Girbau. This financing is shown as part of the long-term debt on the balance sheet.

> Under long-term assets, Lazybones shows the property plant and equipment for the four new company stores, but nothing for franchise support.

10.5 Statement of Cash Flows

Exhibit 10.9 Simple Five-Year Statement of Cash Flows

	Year 1	Year 2	Year 3	Year 4	Year 5
Cash flows from operations	-$458,721	$98,293	$741,905	$1,517,209	$2,151,099
Cash used by investing activities	-$244,400	$0	$0	$0	$0
Cash used by financing activities	$775,494	-$60,057	-$65,691	-$71,853	-$46,450
Net increase (decrease) in cash	$72,373	$38,236	$676,214	$1,445,356	$2,104,649
Cash at beginning of the period	$65,800	$138,173	$176,408	$852,623	$2,297,979
Cash at end of period	$138,173	$176,408	$852,623	$2,297,979	$4,402,628

Most Lazybones customers will pay up front for a semester or year with a credit card, and most customers sign up in the first month or two of a semester. This results in the company being flush with cash early in a semester, and then slowly spending the cash on delivering services. Nevertheless, we intend to borrow money (about $500,000) to open new company stores, and to pay for the heavy administrative burden associated with entering franchising. This borrowing is reflected in the first month of the balance sheet and cash flow statement (Exhibit 10.10). Principal and interest payments (all money loaned is assumed to be at 9 percent over seven years) are included throughout the financials.

> As we look at the balance sheet and cash flow statement, we think there needs to be a deeper explanation. Dan notes that they are borrowing about $500,000 to fund growth, but the balance sheet shows $775,494 in year one, and the cash flow statement shows $830,400. We suspect that Dan has $500,000 coming from friends and family to fund growing the corporate infrastructure, and the other debt is for equipment for the new company-owned stores and is provided by Continental-Girbau. But this needs clarification.

> For a new venture and one undergoing rapid growth, it is imperative to show cash flow monthly for the first two years. If the company runs out of cash, it is out of business. For new venture projections, the maximum negative cash flow (preinvestment) often equals the amount of capital, staged by milestones and cash needs, the venture will need to raise.

Exhibit 10.10 Detailed Five-Year Statement of Cash Flows (two years month to month)

Part A: Year 1

	July	Aug	Sept	Oct	Nov	Dec	Semester
Cash flows from operations	($78,489)	($68,332)	$7,374	($85,111)	($92,794)	($49,735)	($367,086)
Investing activities							
Purchase of equipment	($244,400)	$0	$0	$0	$0	$0	($244,400)
Cash used by investing activities	($244,400)	$0	$0	$0	$0	$0	($244,400)
Financing activities							
Borrowing	$830,400	$0	$0	$0	$0	$0	$830,400
Principal payments	($4,390)	($4,423)	($4,456)	($4,489)	($4,523)	($4,557)	($26,838)
Cash used by financing activities	$826,010	($4,423)	($4,456)	($4,489)	($4,523)	($4,557)	$803,562
Net increase (decrease) in cash	$503,121	($72,754)	$2,918	($89,601)	($97,317)	($54,292)	$192,076
Cash at beginning of the period	$65,800	$568,921	$496,166	$499,085	$409,484	$312,167	$65,800

	Jan	Feb	Mar	Apr	May	Jun	Semester	Year 1
Cash flows from operations	$123,130	($81,538)	($104,466)	($100,951)	$165,302	($93,112)	($91,635)	($458,721)
Investing activities								
Purchase of equipment								
Cash used by investing activities	$0	$0	$0	$0	$0	$0	$0	($244,400)
Financing activities	$0	$0	$0	$0	$0	$0	$0	($244,400)
Borrowing								
Principal payments	$0	$0	$0	$0	$0	$0	$0	$830,400
Cash used by financing activities	($4,591)	($4,626)	($4,660)	($4,695)	($4,730)	($4,766)	($28,069)	($54,906)
Net Increase (decrease) in cash	($4,591)	($4,626)	($4,660)	($4,695)	($4,730)	($4,766)	($28,069)	$775,494
Cash at beginning of the period	$118,539	($86,163)	($109,126)	($105,646)	$160,572	($97,878)	($119,703)	$72,373
Cash at end of period	$257,876	$376,414	$290,251	$181,125	$75,478	$236,050	$257,876	$65,800

Part B: Years 2–5

	July	Aug	Sept	Oct	Nov	Dec	Semester
Cash flows from operations	$57,942	($10,403)	$125,223	($77,652)	($85,950)	($69,852)	($60,692)
Investing activities							
Purchase of equipment	$0	$0	$0	$0	$0	$0	$0
Cash used by investing activities	$0	$0	$0	$0	$0	$0	$0
Financing activities							
Borrowing	$0						
Principal payments	($4,802)	($4,838)	($4,874)	($4,910)	($4,947)	($4,984)	($29,356)
Cash used by financing activities	($4,802)	($4,838)	($4,874)	($4,910)	($4,947)	($4,984)	($29,356)
Net Increase (decrease) in cash	$53,140	($15,241)	$120,349	($82,562)	($90,897)	($74,837)	($90,048)
Cash at beginning of the period	$138,173	$191,313	$176,072	$296,421	$213,859	$122,962	$138,173
Cash at end of period	$191,313	$176,072	$296,421	$213,859	$122,962	$48,125	$48,125

Jan	Feb	Mar	Apr	May	Jun	Semester	Year 2	Year 3	Year 4	Year 5
$237,873	($53,879)	($92,528)	($81,192)	$273,298	($124,588)	$158,985	$98,293	$741,905	$1,517,209	$2,151,099
$0	$0	$0	$0	$0	$0	$0	$0	$0	$0	$0
$0	$0	$0	$0	$0	$0	$0	$0	$0	$0	$0
$5,022)	($5,059)	($5,097)	($5,136)	($5,174)	($5,213)	($30,702)	($60,057)	($65,691)	($71,853)	($46,450)
($5,022)	($5,059)	($5,097)	($5,136)	($5,174)	($5,213)	($30,702)	($60,057)	($65,691)	($71,853)	($46,450)
$232,852	($58,939)	($97,625)	($86,327)	$268,124	($129,801)	$128,283	$38,236	$676,214	$1,445,356	$2,104,649
$48,125	$280,977	$222,038	$124,413	$38,085	$306,209	$48,125	$138,173	$176,408	$852,623	$2,297,979
$280,977	$222,038	$124,413	$38,085	$306,209	$176,408	$176,408	$176,408	$852,623	$2,297,979	$4,402,628

Appendices: Adding Bells and Whistles

The appendices can include anything that you think adds further validation to your concept but doesn't fit or is too large to insert in the main parts of the plan. Common inclusions would be one-page résumés of key team members, articles that feature your venture, technical specifications, and so forth. Lazybones included a brochure and other marketing materials that it uses to secure customers. Due to space constraints, these appendices aren't included within this book.

Chapter Summary

Financial projections are an art. You can never precisely predict the future, but you need to anticipate what can happen. Financial projections help you gauge the attractiveness of the opportunity. What is the profit potential? How might the company grow? What does this mean for you, your team, your employees, and your investors? In summary, financial projections are the numbers equivalent of the story you have articulated in the rest of the plan. Just like the written plan, the financial statements need revisiting and refining as you learn more about the opportunity. We believe it is imperative for you, the lead entrepreneur, to own the numbers. If you rely on others, you won't be able to make strong decisions on how to proceed or convincingly raise money that you need to get started. So, although building and understanding financial statements can require effort for those of you who are less proficient in numbers, the time you take to familiarize yourself with the financials is time well spent.

11 CONCLUSION

Lazybones Epilogue

The Lazybones plan that we used throughout this book is an actual plan produced by the entrepreneur trying to grow his business beyond a lifestyle firm. This is the first iteration of the plan and likely quite different from the current plan that the team is implementing. Since the writing of the plan, Lazybones has opened and closed a new store near the University of Connecticut (UConn) and then subsequently opened a store near the University of Delaware. Dan noted that they tried to open UConn too quickly and Dan and Joel (the corporate staff) were overextended bringing Boston and Boulder up to speed. The main difficulty in opening any store is making sure you have the right store management team in place and that the team has the appropriate training. Adding UConn so quickly after the new locations in Boulder and Boston made it difficult for Joel and Dan to properly oversee the UConn operation. This speaks to some of the comments we added to the plan regarding developing the appropriate infrastructure around franchise support and training (even though the initial stores are company owned). Once the Boston and Boulder locations were operating efficiently and after they closed UConn, Lazybones opened the Delaware store. Thus, at this point two years out from the original plan, Lazybones has five locations. You'll note that this is well behind plan as Dan and Joel had expected to have eight company stores and to start franchising during this second year. It is common for entrepreneurs to be overoptimistic in how quickly they can grow their business. Like all entrepreneurs, implementing the business plan is a learning experience and Dan and Joel have revised their roll-out to better reflect the time to get new stores up and running. As of the writing of this chapter, Lazybones looks on track, albeit a bit slower than expected.

During each major draft, the entrepreneur's sophistication in describing the concept and opportunity improves. It is useful to map how the business has evolved over time. Below are the major changes (items 1–5 precede the plan illustrated in this book, While items 6-8 are included in the business plan in this book):

1. Starts a laundry service in Wisconsin with former college roommate. Has rudimentary plan, but learns much on the job.
2. Refines the business over six years and then opens second location in Syracuse.
3. In 2003, Dan moves to Boston and runs the Syracuse unit remotely.
4. While earning his MBA on a part-time basis, Dan learns about franchising.
5. In 2008, adds two more locations in Boulder and Boston. Develops plan to grow the company through franchising.
6. In 2009 as part of the franchising strategy, they open a company location in Connecticut.
7. In 2010, close down UConn, but open U. of Delaware.
8. Currently identifying future company-owned locations and putting together their franchising memorandum.

While planning is valuable in that it helps the entrepreneurs gain a deeper understanding of their business, it is critical to put that planning into action. Each of these iterations suggests that Dan has gained a much deeper understanding of how to best shape this opportunity and grow his business. Based upon the success of his first two stores and interest from happy customers about franchising the concept, Dan believes that Lazybones has the potential to be a national brand. Planning has helped him understand how to go about franchising. Too many times entrepreneurs fall into one of two traps. First, they "just do it" and try to learn as they go. While this can work, it often leads to costly mistakes. Alternatively, would-be entrepreneurs try to anticipate everything in advance and don't implement their plan until it is "perfect." The problem is that no matter how rigorous your planning process, no plan is ever perfect. These would-be entrepreneurs are often too paralyzed to act on their plan. The key is to find the proper balance between planning and action to improve your chances of success. Based upon Dan's success to date, he appears to have the proper balance.

As part of Dan's planning process, he has been actively talking to experts in franchising. In addition to taking classes, Dan has consulted with Les Charm, an expert on growing companies and franchising. Dan also worked closely with a mentor, Jim Bardis, former chief operating officer and vice president of company-owned stores for ExecuTrain, a company that provides business training services. Dan teamed up with Joel because he recognized a weakness in his own skill set. Joel had over 10 years of leadership experience with companies ranging in size from $12 million to $50 million. Considering that Lazybones would like to hit these revenue targets, it makes sense to bring in someone with operating experience in larger companies. Dan has also networked with other people with successful experience in franchising.

As the foregoing example illustrates, entrepreneurs who talk and network not only improve their vision but also find potential partners and advisers. Who should you talk to? The list starts with the smartest people in the industry. Who are the world-class experts that you will emulate or even hope to exceed? It includes potential customers, distributors, vendors, advisers, mentors, and even competitors. Very early in the process you should define who your core customer is in terms of demographics (age, gender, income, etc.) and psychographics (what motivates the person to buy). During such interactions, Dan has learned how to best reach his core customer, the college student, by partnering with the university to become a preferred provider. In this way, the university includes information on Lazybones in communications with students (users) and their parents (payers). By talking with a friend and seeing what has worked, Dan has a set of metrics that helps him identify and prioritize universities to expand to, including high tuition, students with high disposable income, and a large student population. These conversations also fostered advisers.

Dan has also spent considerable time fostering relationships with suppliers, most notably Continental-Girbau, who supplies Lazybones with washing machines, dryers, and other critical equipment for laundries.

This strong relationship has led to a promise by Continental-Girbau to provide debt financing to Lazybones and its franchisees for the equipment to open new stores. One of the most difficult tasks that an entrepreneur faces is financing growth. Using a combination of equipment financing along with the franchisees' capital to build new stores will help Lazybones secure the capital it needs for its aggressive growth strategy. However, Continental-Girbau also provides Lazybones with intelligence. The supplier can help Dan keep abreast of the latest on new equipment, such as energy- and water-saving machines to understand the tradeoff between the likely higher price and the savings from lower energy and water bills. Continental-Girbau probably also sells to current and potential competitors. Thus a strong relationship may lead to intelligence on who is entering new locations and, maybe even more valuable, who is exiting locations (closing down). Although vendors would never divulge trade secrets—nor should you press them to—you can gain insight into how your competitors operate. If you have an innovative product—one that you believe nobody else has—you may learn through vendors of "stealth" competitors; companies that are in the prelaunch period who have yet to sell product or service. Vendors are often knowledgeable of other suppliers you might need, or what distribution channels might work. They can also provide a different perspective on what your customer wants. It is never too early to start talking to potential vendors.

Dan can also use his contacts at universities to gain valuable intelligence. In the case of Lazybones, universities are basically their distribution partners because they connect the company to its end users. Universities have a deep knowledge of their students and their parents and can help Dan better understand his end customer. Even though Lazybones has a long operating history, customers in Wisconsin and Syracuse may not be exactly the same as students from universities in other parts of the country. Keeping close connection to these universities helps Dan not only pick the best locations for growth but also to modify Lazybones services to best meet their needs. Likewise, you should keep in close contact with your distribution partners, who can provide you with insight into your end user.

Like all successful entrepreneurs Dan has done an excellent job of broadening his cast of advisers beyond experts in his field (franchising). He has leveraged all of his business school professors (including us) by meeting with us outside of class and even after graduation. Dan has used his network to identify a lawyer who helped in contracting with vendors and providers and also helped identify key issues to include in the Franchise Disclosure Document for lower fees than if he had arranged it through the phone book. Entrepreneurs who engage constituencies are more likely to move the business forward than are paranoid entrepreneurs who believe everybody is out to steal their idea.

It is even possible to talk to your competitors by attending trade shows. As soon as Dan started to investigate franchising as a growth strategy, he started attending trade shows. Through these events he met many entrepreneurs who were trying to franchise their concepts, as well as potential franchisees. This helped him better understand the franchise model. What kinds of fees to charge, what kinds of support the franchisees expect, how much it costs to support franchisees, and so forth. At trade shows, you'll find that people are open about their businesses, even competitors. As such, you can gain deep insight into your competition's business and strategy. The key is to view the business planning process as one of gathering information that will help you move the business forward and succeed.

As we are writing this book (fall of 2010), Lazybones continues to make progress toward growing their business. As noted, they have five company stores and are on track to start franchising later this year. They have streamlined their reporting mechanisms between the stores and corporate, and they have learned how to hire managers at these different stores. Business planning will help you gain that deep understanding necessary to convincingly articulate your vision and get buy-in from investors, customers, team members, and so forth.

Next Steps If You Need Funding

Once you have a strong draft of your business plan, you are in a better position to seek outside funding. However, most investors, whether they are venture capitalists, angels, friends, or family, do not want to see your full, completed plan, at least not initially. What they want is often a dehydrated plan (5–10 pages) and 5–10 PowerPoint slides. Many investors will ask you to email them the summary and slides in advance of them possibly asking you in for a meeting. They want something short and concise to get a sense of the opportunity (is the market large and growing? does the entrepreneur have an exciting and sensible approach to the market? etc.), a good sense of the team (are you capable of executing on the opportunity?), and how the investment will help you move the business to the next level. If the investors are *excited* after reading your summary and reviewing your slides, they will likely ask you in to discuss the opportunity. Think of the stand-alone summary and PowerPoint slides as a hook. You are trying to entice the investors to learn more. If the meeting goes well and the investor is still interested, she may ask for the full plan. Many investors use the business plan as a roadmap to conduct due diligence—to investigate whether your claims are valid or just a pipe dream. But before you can get there, you need to hook the investor.

The dehydrated business plan is derived from your full business plan.[1] First and foremost, you need to add a cover page, similar to the one that you have included on the business plan. Add visuals such as product pictures, competitor maps, customer profiles, and so forth. In addition to filling out details on all the subsections of the plan, provide as much information on the team as possible. Harkening back to the old adage that investors prefer to back A-level teams with B ideas versus B teams with A ideas, you need to convince them that you can execute on the opportunity. In the appendix, we evaluate Lazybones's slides. If Dan were seeking outside investors, he would send the slides along with an expanded executive summary to prime the investors for a potential meeting.

Creating PowerPoint slides is a valuable exercise in that it forces you to think about your opportunity visually. The 12 or so slides should cover the following areas:

1. Cover page showing product picture, company name, and contact information
2. Opportunity description emphasizing customer problem or need that you hope to solve
3. Your product or service illustrating how it solves the customer's problem, with some details (as needed) to better describe your product
4. Competition overview

---

[1]Remember in Chapter 2 we suggested that the first step you might do is write a dehydrated plan because it is a good document to share with team members and other trusted advisers who can help you develop your business. The dehydrated plan you write at the end of the business planning process is much more articulate than the previous version. It has the ability to hook investors.

5. Your entry and growth strategy showing how you get into the industry and then grow
6. Overview of your business model, describing how you make money and how much it costs to support those sales
7. Team description
8. Current status with timeline
9. Summary including how much you need and how that money will be used

One mistake that entrepreneurs often make in creating their Power-Point slides is using too much text. Bullet point slides are easy to create, but they aren't as compelling as pictures. A picture is truly worth a thousand words. So your challenge is to substitute visuals for words whenever possible. The appendix of the book will also illustrate PowerPoint slides for Lazybones. It should be noted that these 16 slides include "build" components and therefore appear to be greater than 16 slides.

Beyond the Business Plan

There is much debate about the value of a business plan. We even proclaim that the plan will be obsolete as soon as it comes off the press! Some have suggested that 5 or 10 PowerPoint slides, a dehydrated plan, or an executive summary is all that is needed. These are important extracts from the business plan, but the argument about whether you need a business plan or not is a red herring. Most of the debate is really about communicating the contents of the plan, not about business planning itself. This book helps you travel along a very personal entrepreneurial journey in a manner that will focus your energies. The true value of crafting a business plan is to impose the discipline that allows you to become an expert about your industry and your idea for making that industry better. Ultimately, the business planning process helps you shape your ideas into concrete, executable opportunities that create value. This process, the hard work of new venture due diligence and articulation, is a learnable skill that makes you a better entrepreneur. Remember, the deep understanding of your opportunity is the competitive advantage you will need to push the odds of success in your favor. At the same time it will also help you raise money, recruit key management, secure vendors, and attract customers.

Although this book lays out the business plan as a sequential process, you must remember it is iterative. Writing one section has implications on the other sections of the plan, and you will find yourself revisiting those sections continuously. That is why it doesn't matter that the business plan is obsolete the minute it comes out of the printer. Harkening back to Chapter 1 where we talked about the Timmons Model, the planning process helps you do the following:

1. Gauge the nature of the opportunity
2. Shape that opportunity and create a plan to launch and grow the business
3. Enhance your ability to articulate the value-creating potential of your company

Having worked with hundreds of entrepreneurs throughout the years, we are always impressed at the tangible growth in clarity of the entrepreneur's vision during the business planning process. The process forces you to ask and answer important questions. It helps you identify the critical assumptions, or leaps of faith, that must occur for this business to succeed. Once you understand those assumptions, you can take steps to reduce the uncertainty around them. More knowledge will enhance your chances of success.

Conclusion

Welcome to the entrepreneurial revolution. We hope that you have found this book useful as you embark on your entrepreneurial endeavor. By going through the business planning process, you will improve your chances of success. The process and the discipline put you in charge of evaluating and shaping choices and initiating action that makes sense, rather than letting things just happen. Having a longer-term sense of direction is highly motivating. It is also extremely helpful in determining when to say no (which is much harder than saying yes) and can temper impulsive hunches with a more thoughtful strategic purpose.

When you have successfully launched your business you will contribute to the country's economic vitality. Your business will likely create jobs not just for you but for others. Your business may well be a lasting legacy that outlives you. Remember to think big. Companies that grow will survive and prosper. Because of their innovative nature and competitive breakthroughs, entrepreneurial ventures have demonstrated a remarkable capacity to invent new paradigms of organization and management. They have abandoned the organizational practices and structures typical of the industrial giants from the post–World War II era to the 1990s. The world needs big problems solved and has relied on entrepreneurs to find those solutions. Think of Henry Ford, Thomas Watson (IBM), Bill Gates, Mark Zuckerberg (Facebook), Sergey Brin and Larry Page (Google), or Home Depot's Arthur Blank. Your business may not ever reach the size of the aforementioned ones (nor may you even have such aspirations), but you will have a lasting impact on your family and community. Enjoy the trip.

Appendices

Quick Screen Exercise

I. Market- and Margin-Related Issues

Criterion	Higher Potential	Lower Potential
Need/want/problem	Identified	Unfocused
Customers	Reachable and receptive	Unreachable/loyal to others
Payback to users	< 1 year	> 3 years
Value added or created	Investor realizable returns 40% +	Investor realizable returns < 20%
Market size	$50–$100 million	< $10 million or +1 billion
Market growth rate	+20%	< 20%, contracting
Gross margin	40%+ and durable	< 20% and fragile
Overall potential:		
1. Market	Higher _____ avg _____ lower	
2. Margins	Higher _____ avg _____ lower	

II. Competitive Advantages

	Higher Potential	Lower Potential
Fixed and variable costs	Highest >>>>>>>>>>>>>>>> lowest	
Degree of control	Stronger >>>>>>>>>>>>>>> weaker	
Prices and cost		
Channels of supply and distribution		
Barriers to entry	Strong >>>>>>>>>>>>>>>>> none	
Proprietary advantage		
Lead time advantage (product, technology, people, resources, location)		
Service chain		
Contractual advantage		
Contacts and networks		
Overall potential		
1. Costs	Higher _____avg_____ lower	
2. Channel	Higher _____avg_____ lower	
3. Barriers to entry	Higher _____avg_____ lower	
4. Timing	Higher _____avg_____ lower	

III. Value Creation and Realization Issues

	Higher Potential	**Lower Potential**
Profit after tax	10–15% or more and durable	< 5%; fragile
Time to break even	< 2 years	> 3 years
Time to positive cash flow	< 2 years	> 3 years
Return on investment potential	40–70% +, durable	< 20%, fragile
Value	High strategic value	Low strategic value
Capitalization requirements	Low–moderate; fundable	Very high; difficult to fund
Exit mechanism	Initial public offering, acquisition	Undefined; illiquid investment

Overall value creation potential

1. Timing   Higher _____avg_____ lower

2. Profit/free cash flow   Higher _____avg_____ lower

3. Exit/liquidity   Higher _____avg_____ lower

IV. Overall Potential

	Go	**No Go**	**Go, if…**
1. Margins and markets			
2. Competitive advantages			
3. Value creation and realization			
4. Fit: "Opportunity" + "Resources" + "Team"			
5. Risk/reward/balance			
6. Timing			
7. Other compelling issues: must know or likely to fail			

     a.

     b.

     c.

     d.

     e.

2 Business Planning Guide Exercise

Name:

Venture:

Data:

Step 1: Segment Information into Key Sections

Establish priorities for each section, including individuals responsible and due dates for drafts and the final version. When you segment your information, it is vital to keep in mind that the plan needs to be logically integrated, and that information should be consistent. Note that since the market opportunity section is the heart and soul of the plan, it may be the most difficult section to write; but it is best to assign it a high priority and to begin working there first. Remember to include in the list such tasks as printing.

Section or Task	Priority	Person(s) Responsible	Date to Begin	First Draft Due Date	Date Completed or Final Version Due Date

Step 2: List Tasks That Need to Be Completed

Devise an overall schedule for preparing the plan by assigning priority, persons responsible, and due dates to each task necessary to complete the plan. It is helpful to break larger items (fieldwork to gather customer and competitor intelligence, trade show visits, etc.) into small, more manageable components (such as phone calls required before a trip can be taken) and to include the components as a task. *Be as specific as possible.*

Task	Priority	Person(s) Responsible	Date to Begin	Date of Completion

Step 3: Combine the List of Segments and the List of Tasks to Create a Calendar

In combining your lists, consider whether anything has been omitted and whether you have been realistic in what people can do, when they can do it, what needs to be done, and so forth. To create your calendar, place an X in the week when the task is to be started and an X in the week it is to be completed and then connect the Xs. When you have placed all tasks on the calendar, look carefully again for conflicts or lack of realism. In particular, evaluate whether team members are overscheduled.

Task	Week														
	1	2	3	4	5	6	7	8	9	10	11	12	13	14	15

Step 4: A Framework to Develop and Write a Business Plan

While preparing your own plan, you will most likely want to consider sections in a different order from the one presented in this book. Also, when you integrate your sections into your final plan, you may choose to present material somewhat differently. The key is to make it *your* plan.

3 Sample Presentation

Nice clean opening slide with visual that captures the essence of the business. Also note that they have their contact information right on the slide.

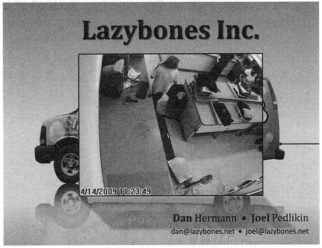

This is a build onto the first slide that shows how they remotely monitor various stores via webcam. As you read the business plan, clients can also monitor the stores.

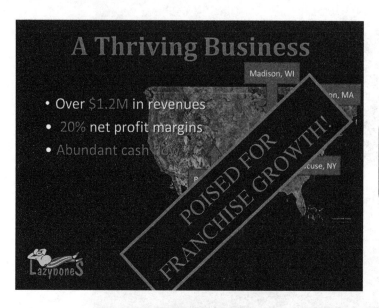

Nice slide in that it captures the highlights of the business. Shows the four locations and some key company metrics. This is the Hook.

Considering the success the team has had to date, it makes sense to highlight them early in the presentation. If you have an inexperienced team, it might appear later. Although, we like visuals, we'd also like a bit of detail on what each brings to the company. An effective way to do that is a grid that shows key skills needed accross the top, team members down the side, and then checkmarks as to who on the team possessess those skills.

There is a playfulness to the slides that can be endearing if it is a reflection of the team spirit. But be careful to take success seriously.

Industry in Depth

U.S. Laundry and Dry Cleaning Industry = $1 Billion

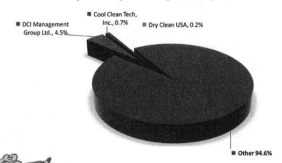

For the next Three slides, these were build slides (meaning in effect only one slide of the presentation). We like how they capture in a very visual way, the essence of the industry and why this is an opportunity. In this slide, for instance, they illustrate that the industry is highly fragmented (versus dominated by one or two large competitiors). This suggests that there is an opportunity to create a national brand.

NO big *laundry* players

Industry in Depth

U.S. Franchising = $90 Billion

This slide captures the power of franchising and in particular shows that the segment of personal services (where Lazybones is focused) is the fastest growing.

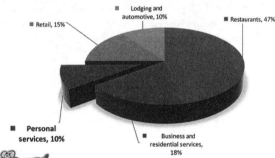

Personal services is *fastest growing* segment at 53%

Industry in Depth

U.S. Four-Year Colleges

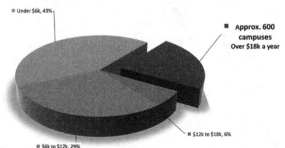

- Approx. 600 campuses Over $18k a year

This slide illustrates the target market. Large campuses with high tuition. Shows that there are 600 potential sites for the franchise.

1,600 campuses with enrollment over 2,500 students

End Customers

"U.S. college freshmen come from families with a median income 60% higher than the national average."
~ UCLA Newsroom

Nice drill down to the user (students) and buyer (parents). This reinforces their experience and textured understanding of the market.

Students

• **Customer Service and Marketing**
Tailored to each separately

Parents

Competitive Advantages

- **We do the work ourselves**
- **Laser-focused on college students**
- **Combination of laundry and storage**
- **Custom operational systems**

Having integrated component of competitive advantages in advantageous. They might reinforce the statement "We do the work ourselves" = quality systems.

Positioning Chart

We really like position maps that illustrate how your firm stacks up on two key criteria. In this case, the map is geared toward potential franchisees and why they might choose Lazybones over another alternative.

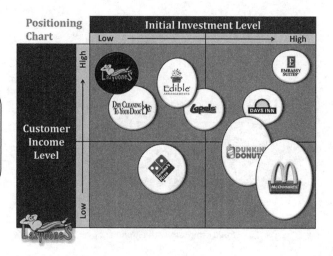

Advantages to Franchisees

- Low upfront out-of-pocket ~ $100k
- Rapid return on investment
- Excellent cash flow
- Custom integrated business systems

Some more details that highlight the power of this business.

One campus franchise fee $35k
Royalty rate 7%

Marketing to Franchisees

Integrate with current marketing efforts

- 8 campuses = 300,000+ students and parents across the country
- Numerous inquiries WITHOUT prior effort

This slide shows how Lazbones hopes to acquire potential franchisees. We would recommend adding that there is the potential for 600+ locations. That sets up the next slides to say how Lazybones will achieve market dominance.

Additional marketing

- Web marketing
- Active with franchising organizations (International Franchise Association)
- Target likely interest groups

Five-Year Growth Plan

- Four new company-owned stores by Jan 2010
- Selling franchises by Aug 2010
- 60 franchises by 2015

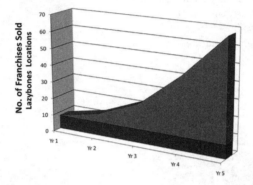

We like the graphical representation of how Lazybones will grow over time. Note that the blue bar represents the eight company-owned stores and the red represents new franchisees.

Five-Year Growth Plan

We like how Lazybones benchmarks its growth against other franchise operations. Here, they have suggested that they are growing slower, which might make this more realistic. Of course, an investor might question why they aren't growing faster.

- Four new company-owned stores by Jan 2010
- Selling franchises by Aug 2010
- 60 franchises by 2015

Franchise Start-up Comparison

System4 (dry-cleaning)

Edible Arrangements

Fetch! Pet Care

Lazybones

Unit Economics

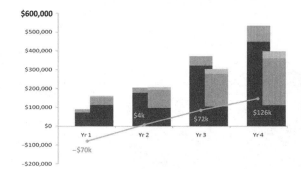

This slide suggests that the stores break-even in the second year. That could prove problematic for some franchisees. Investors will not be concerned.

Company-wide Economics

This graph shows how the total Lazybones company operates by aggregating all its stores (both company and franchisees).

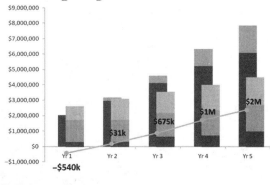

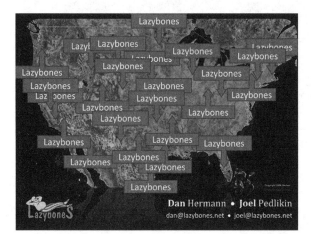

This map suggests potential growth. It is very visual in that the Lazybones arrows come up in a timed sequence to show the growth trajectory.

Cash Need

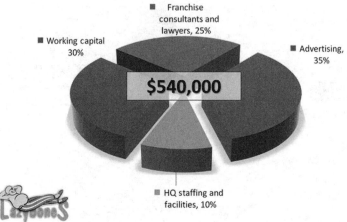

■ Franchise consultants and lawyers, 25%

■ Working capital 30%

■ Advertising, 35%

$540,000

■ HQ staffing and facilities, 10%

While we like how they are illustrating the financing needed and how it will be used, a table with actual amounts attributed to each activity (rather than percentages) would be easier to understand.

Franchise Customers

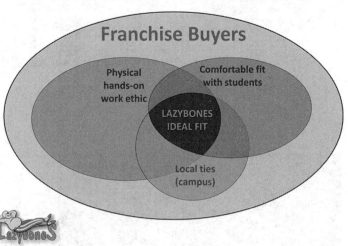

This is their conclusion slide geared toward the audience (potential franchisees), reiterating main points raised in the previous slide. It is important to restate the three to five main points you want your audience to remember.

Franchise Buyers

Physical hands-on work ethic

Comfortable fit with students

LAZYBONES IDEAL FIT

Local ties (campus)

Index

About the Authors

Andrew Zacharakis is the John H. Muller, Jr., Chair in Entrepreneurship at Babson College and director of the Babson College Entrepreneurship Research Conference.

Stephen Spinelli is the founder of Jiffy Lube International and president of Philadelphia University.

Jeffry A. Timmons, D.B.A., was the Franklin W. Olin Distinguished Professor of Entrepreneurship at Babson College and author of the *Inc.* top ten book *New Venture Creation.*